The Island of St Patrick

THE ISLAND OF ST PATRICK

*Church and ruling dynasties
in Fingal and Meath, 400–1148*

Ailbhe MacShamhráin

EDITOR

FOUR COURTS PRESS

Set in 11pt on 14pt Adobe Garamond by
Carrigboy Typesetting Services, County Cork, for
FOUR COURTS PRESS LTD
7 Malpas Street, Dublin 8, Ireland
e-mail: info@four-courts-press.ie
and in North America for
FOUR COURTS PRESS
c/o ISBS, 920 N.E. 58th Avenue, Suite 300, Portland, OR 97213

A catalogue record for this title is available
from the British Library.

ISBN 1–85182–867–2

Printed in Great Britain by
MPG Books, Bodmin, Cornwall.

Contents

Contents

Foreword

Any attempt at sketching the history of the first millennium of Christianity in Ireland – an island which the world at large associates with St Patrick – is a bold venture. However, the area of Fingal, and adjacent parts of Co. Meath (the ancient kingdom of Brega), present us with a unique opportunity to study the process in microcosm. Church Island, known locally as Inis Phádraig or St Patrick's Island, is one of the five Skerries off-shore islands where, according to legend, St Patrick kept a goat which was captured and eaten by the local people. In reparation, the parish church in Skerries features a statue of St Patrick near its doorway and rather than letting sleeping goats lie, the people of Skerries have immortalized the story underneath on a bronze plaque.

Church Island has an importance beyond the legend that the saint made his first landfall there on his return to Ireland in his mission to preach Christianity to fifth-century Irish tribes. The island ruins is almost inaccessible, and as a result it is one of county Dublin's least visited church-sites. There was, apparently, an early monastery on the island, raided and burnt in AD 798 by the Vikings who, according to accounts, seized a richly ornamented shrine containing relics of St Do-Chonna. The Augustinians established a priory on the island some time before the intervention of the Normans in 1169 and these are the ruins that you see today. The most momentous event in the history of the island – and a milestone in the ecclesiastical history of Ireland as a whole – took place in 1148, when a synod of bishops and clergy gathered there under the guidance of St Malachy, then papal legate. Years ago cattle kept the grass down and were given shelter through the building of a temporary roof over the nave. Now, they too have gone, so that the luxuriating summer vegetation makes walking the island as difficult as landing on it, and provides almost undisturbed nesting facilities for the sea-birds.

Fr Leo Quinlan, parish priest of St Patrick's Parish, decided to place the Skerries folklore in an archaeological and historical context. He enlisted the enthusiastic support of local archaeologist and historian, Dr

Michael Ryan, Director of the Chester Beatty Library, to initiate an enquiry into St Patrick from archaeological, historical and spiritual perspectives. With this goal in mind the Skerries Patrician Millennium Committee was formed whose efforts resulted in a three day conference on 'St Patrick and Early Christianity in Fingal *c.*400 to 1200 AD' held in Skerries between 19 and 21 May 2000. As chairman, I would like to thank all the members of the committee, and computer-specialist Victor Reij, for their very generous commitment in making the conference a success and the people of Skerries and Fingal for their support in the project.

Eugene A. Coyle,
Chairman, Skerries Patrician Millennium Project
The Feast of Mac-Cuilinn of Lusk, 6 September 2003.

THE SKERRIES PATRICIAN MILLENNIUM PROJECT (1998–2001)

Committee
Eugene A. Coyle (Chairman)
Fr Leo Quinlan, PP (Hon. Secretary)
Declan O'Sullivan (Hon. Treasurer)
Dr Peter Harbison (Archaeological advisor)
Dr Michael Ryan (Archaeological advisor)
Michael Lynch (Fingal County Council)
Stephanie Bourke (Skerries Mills)
Marie Baker (Skerries Historical Society)
Terry McCoy (Red Bank Restaurant)
The Revd Kieran Coghlan
Steven Hope
Dr Ailbhe MacShamhráin (Medievalist, Conference Coordinator)

Sponsors and patrons
Allied Irish Bank, Skerries
Community College Skerries
Dublin Institute of Technology (Bolton Street, Dublin)
Fingal County Council
The Heritage Council
Luke Moriarty
Red Bank Restaurant
Rural Dublin LEADER Company Ltd.
Skerries Historical Society
St Patrick's Parish

Preface

With entry into the third millennium, it seemed opportune to reflect on church and society in Ireland and to re-examine aspects of our heritage from the Early Christian experience. Such thinking lay behind the Skerries Patrician Conference, held in summer 2000. Funding from the Irish Heritage Council and the Rural Dublin LEADER Company Limited, whose assistance is gratefully acknowledged, ultimately made it possible to produce this book – comprised of papers originally prepared for the conference, but substantially re-worked between 2002 and 2003. The general aim of the project was to explore a sequence of themes from the introduction of Christianity into Ireland (popularly associated with St Patrick) to the twelfth-century church reform, which ushered in a new diocesan structure and hierarchy and saw the introduction of Continental religious orders. As remarked in the foreword above, ancient Brega (which includes Fingal and most of Co. Meath) provides an ideal opportunity to examine this process in microcosm. According to the seventh-century hagiographer, Bishop Tírechán, it was at Inis Pátraic (or Church Island), near Skerries, that St Patrick first landed when he returned to evangelize the Irish. It was also at Inis Pátraic that the important reforming synod of 1148 – which established the framework for Ireland's diocesan system – was convened. Between the time of Christianization and that of reform, developments at local level mirrored those within Ireland as a whole in relation to dynastic change and its implications for the church, ecclesiastical settlement, organizational expansion, the growth of religious cults, ecclesiastical architecture and imagery and, following the Viking conflicts, the gradual intergration of Scandinavian settlers into Irish socio-religious structures.

As with most sets of conference proceedings, this is very much a thematic collection but the papers are arranged in a sequence that is broadly chronological from the fifth century to the twelfth. In the first contribution here, an updated version of the keynote address, Professor Charles Thomas explores the mythologizing of St Patrick's mission (alleged to have begun at Skerries) and how, in the process, the important contribution of the fifth-century Bishop Palladius was 'air-brushed' out of history. As elsewhere, Christianity became established in Ireland within a particular political context, and Dr Edel Bhreathnach examines the dynastic structure of Brega (Co. Meath) in the Early Christian period, revealing a network of minor dynasties that underlay the Uí Néill hegemony at local level. As an example of ecclesiastical settlement, the editor discusses an early (possibly sixth- or seventh-century) site at Grange, near Skerries, where a large enclosure has recently (2003) been discovered, and considers the probable identity of its local patron saint. In the light of claims to ecclesiastical primacy advanced by Armagh, at least by the seventh century, Dr Catherine Swift evaluates the testimony of Bishop Tírechán regarding Patrician churches in the Co. Meath area, and seeks to locate them in the landscape.

In parallel with such aggrandisement in ecclesiastical politics, cult diffusion proceeded apace; here, Cormac Bourke focuses on St Columba, whose cult is closely associated with Fingal and Meath, and re-evaluates his status as an exile. Turning to the visual arts, Dr Peter Harbison traces Patrician imagery from medieval times to the present, with particular reference to Fingal. It happens that the area of our concern experienced Viking raids from the end of the eighth century, and the resulting socio-political trauma presumably had implications for settlement and for dynastic ambitions alike. On the basis of their recent survey, Dr Michael Ryan and his co-authors reassess antiquarian accounts of the remains on Church Island (St Patrick's Island) and consider indications of structures, adjacent to the surviving (twelfth-century) ruin, of apparently earlier – perhaps ninth or tenth century – date. That very period, as discussed by the editor in his second contribution, was marked by increasingly overt connections between ecclesiastical centres and local or regional dynasties – as instanced by the example of Inis Pátraic and Máel-Finnia, king of Brega, against a background of parallel dynastic links with Lusk. The gradual conversion to Christianity of the Dublin Scandinavians, from the tenth century, led to the adoption of Continental and Irish saints' cults – including those of Patrick and Columba – as considered by here by Dr Howard Clarke. Finally, Martin Holland revisits the twelfth-century church reform, and examines the key role in this process of the synod of Inis Pátraic – convened there, he argues, precisely because it was believed that the mission of St Patrick (who was credited with the conversion of Ireland) had begun there. The wheel has thus been brought full circle, from the alleged role of St Patrick's Island in the conversion-process to its historical role in the church reform.

It remains for me, as editor, to place on record my sincere thanks to each and every one of the contributors. All concerned, having initially produced a fine selection of conference-papers, painstakingly reworked and updated their submissions and maintained great patience with a project which (for reasons too complex to explain here) was rather more protracted than it should have been. Sadly, one of the conference-speakers, the ever-popular Leo Swan, did not live to see the project into its publication stage. His passing was a great loss to Irish archaeology. As always with such projects, there are many who helped 'behind the scenes' and who facilitated the publication in various ways – too many to name individually. However, in addition to those acknowledged by Eugene Coyle in his capacity as Chairman of the Skerries Patrician Millennium Project, it is right and fitting to record our collective thanks to the staff at Dúchas, Oifig na Logainmneacha, the Ordnance Survey and the National Museum. Finally, a special word of thanks to Michael Adams and his team at Four Courts Press, without whose Herculean efforts in the publication of (especially) medieval subject matter, the disciplines of history and archaeology would be very much the poorer.

Ailbhe MacShamhráin

Lá 'le Mac-Cuilinn, 2003.

Abbreviations

AFM	*The Annals of the Four Masters* (otherwise *Annals of the Kingdom of Ireland*), 7 vols. Ed. and trans. John O'Donovan. Dublin, 1851.
Alen's reg.	*Calendar of Archbishop Alen's Register*. Ed. Charles McNeill. Dublin, 1950.
Anc. Rec. Dublin	*Calendar of Ancient Records of Dublin in the possession of the Municipal Corporation*. 19 vols. Ed. J.T. Gilbert and R.M. Gilbert. Dublin, 1889–1944.
Ann. Inisf.	*The Annals of Inisfallen*. Ed. and trans. Seán Mac Airt. Dublin, 1944 (reprint 1988).
Ann. Tig.	'The Annals of Tigernach'. Ed. and trans. Whitley Stokes. *Revue Celtique*, 16–18 (1896–7).
AU	*The Annals of Ulster to AD 1131*. Ed. and trans. Seán Mac Airt and Gearóid Mac Niocaill. Dublin, 1984.
BCC	*Betha Colaim Chille: the Life of Columcille*. Ed. and trans. A. O'Kelleher and G. Schoepperle. Urbana, 1918 (reprint Dublin, 1994).
Bk. Uí Maine	*The Book of Uí Maine, otherwise called 'The Book of the O'Kellys'* Facsimile with introd. By R.A.S. Macalister. Dublin, 1942.
Cal. Doc. Ire.	*Calendar of Documents relating to Ireland, 1171–1251*. (etc.) 5 vols. London, 1875–86.
Chron. Scot.	*Chronicon Scotorum*. Ed. W.M. Hennessy. London, 1866.
Corpus geneal. Hib.	*Corpus Genealogiae Hiberniae*. Ed. Michael A. O'Brien. Dublin, 1962.
Corpus geneal. SS Hib.	*Corpus Genealogiae Sanctorum Hiberniae*. Ed. Pádraig Ó Riain. Dublin, 1988.
Fél. Óeng.	*Félire Óengusso: the Martyrology of Óengus*. Ed. and trans. Whitley Stokes. London, 1905.
ILCC	*The Irish Life of Colum Cille*. Ed. and trans. Máire Herbert in *Iona, Kells and Derry*, 209–88. Oxford, 1988. (reprint Dublin, 1996).
Mart. Donegal	*The Martyrology of Donegal*. Ed. and trans. John O'Donovan, J.H. Todd and W. Reeves. Dublin, 1864.
Mart. Tallaght	*The Martyrology of Tallaght*. Ed. and trans. R.I. Best and H.J. Jackson. London, 1931.
RIA Proc.	*Royal Irish Academy Proceedings*.
RSAI Jn.	*Royal Society of Antiquaries Journal*.
SMR	Sites and Monuments Record.
VC	(Vita (Sancti) Columbae). *Adomnán's Life of Columba*. Ed. and trans. A.O. Anderson and M.O. Anderson. London, 1961.

Palladius and Patrick

CHARLES THOMAS

Many would maintain that it's just not possible to talk of Irish Christian beginnings without mentioning Patrick, a man of singular fascination in his own right; but while he will be considered here, much of the discussion concerns two other early churchmen, one of them Irish, one of them not. I start with Columbanus of Bangor or Luxeuil – often called that, though he was neither born nor died at either of those places; he wrote of himself as both 'Columbanus' and 'Columba' and this has led to confusion with his older contemporary Columba of Iona, Colmcille. We have a number of Columbanus' sermons and letters, written when he was on the Continent, some of them to successive popes. Fourteen hundred years ago, he was writing to Pope Gregory the Great; a long Latin epistle. Like all his work, it displays, not only a mastery of Late Latin composition at his best, but evidence of very considerable reading – here and elsewhere Columbanus tells us from whom he quotes. Dr David Howlett has commented that 'Columban is the first Irishman to have left extant evidence of his ability to marshall a forceful argument in Latin prose, not only competent, but coruscating with wit, irony, and varied verbal punctilio'.[1] This is a man who was born in the mid-sixth century, in a country surrounded by sea that was *extra limites*, had never formed a part of the Roman Empire in the West, and was dominated by another, extremely complex, Indo-European vernacular; Primitive or Archaic Old Irish. And he wrote poems and hymns. If, as now seems, he was the author of *Mundus Iste Transibit*, this may well have been before he left Ireland for the Continent around 590, making him the first Irishman known to have become a Latin author. The long hymn called *Precamur Patrem* in the Antiphonary of Bangor, after slight argument now agreed again to be his work, shows his first comprehensive disposition of varied rhythms, rhyme and alliteration in verse; 'an achievement, the importance

---

1 David Howlett, *The Celtic Latin tradition of Biblical style* (Dublin, 1995), 91.

of which, in every subsequent European literature, one could hardly overstate'.[2] Not bad for a non-Roman barbarian, is it? Nor is there any suggestion, that Columbanus could not have acquired his learning, his assurance, his polish, until he hit Gaul well into his forties. All of this he learned at home.

Let me turn to another of his letters; it was written to Pope Boniface IV, in 613, from Milan, a few years before Columbanus' death at his final little monastery, Bobbio, up in the Appenines. The letter is partly about the ongoing controversy as to how one should calculate the date of Easter – but it is the sort of letter, if you read it carefully, that any pope would squirm with embarrassment, indeed with fury, on receiving it; brilliant, ironic, crushing, but, on the surface, just a very senior churchman (enmeshed for years in both secular and ecclesiastical politics) writing to the most fair Head of all the churches of the whole of Europe, the Shepherd of Shepherds, and so on. Columbanus points out that the Irish method of reckoning Easter goes back to older authority,[3] that new methods are not beyond criticism, and that he, for one, will not tolerate, any implication that the Irish have strayed into error. He writes *Qua fiducia roboratus acsi stimulatus* 'Strengthened and almost goaded by this confidence'. What he tells Boniface is this:

> For all we Irish, inhabitants of the world's edge, are disciples of St Peter and St Paul and of all the disciples who wrote the sacred canon by the Holy Ghost, and we accept nothing, outside the evangelical and apostolic teaching; none has been a heretic, none a Judaizer, none a schismatic; but the Catholic faith, as it was delivered by you first, who are the successors of the holy apostles, is maintained unbroken. *As it was delivered to you first.*[4]

Before he left for the Continent, Columbanus spent some years as the principal lector, the head of the monastic school, at Bangor, Co. Down,

---

2 Ibid., 177. 3 In earlier letters defending the Irish calculation of Easter, to Pope Gregory the Great in 600 and to the synod of Chalon in 603, Columbanus expressly cited the tract 'De Ratione Paschali'; see now D.P. McCarthy & Aidan Breen, *The ante-Nicean Christian Pasch 'De ratione Paschali': the Paschal tract of Anatolius, bishop of Laodicea* (Dublin, 2003), 39, 126, 149. 4 *Sancti Columbani Opera*, ed. and trans. G.S.M. Walker, Scriptores Latini Hibernici, ii (Dublin, 1957), *epistula* v, §3, 38–9.

on the southern shore of Strangford Lough; the strict, the famous, monastery founded by St Comgall about 550, where Columbanus as a youth first took his monastic vows. There is a strong, but resistible, impulse when reading out in English anything written by Columbanus to do so in the voice of Dr Ian Paisley; the more so because there are common aspects to the careers and utterances of these two. It must however be resisted; we do not know much about Columbanus in detail, but a biography written by Jonas at Bobbio soon after his death in 615 tells us that he was, in no sense, a Co. Down man. He was born somewhere in Leinster, around 543, and was already fully educated at home, before, as a teenager, he travelled north to Bangor.[5]

It is what Columbanus does *not* tell us that I find so interesting and I share this with you because it is so seldom pointed out. Nowhere in his surviving writings, not even by implication, and despite the fact that he must have been several decades at Bangor (which is, remember, a mere 23 miles north of Downpatrick) do we find any reference to Patrick; to the presence of fifth-century Christianity, in Ulster, and perhaps a part of Connacht; or to what might be called preserved traditions at Bangor, relating to Patrick's earlier labours. That statement in the letter to Pope Boniface ('as it was delivered by you first') cannot possibly be applied to Patrick. He may have been *episcopus constitutus*, but his return to the Ireland of his youthful captivity can only have been instigated, or permitted, by a synod of the British church (conceivably held at York) and his consecration by existing British bishops. The papacy does not, originally, come into this. And I have to say, in passing, that I do not think Patrick ever landed at St Patrick's Isle, or set foot in Skerries; someone else did.

The year 2005, which is looming uncomfortably close, marks the centenary of publication of Professor J.B. Bury's *The Life of Saint Patrick*. We shall be jolly lucky if we escape a fresh outbreak of *odium Patricianum*, though I don't know how many people have anything dramatically new to say. Count me out, because I jumped the starting gun early, giving the May 1999 Rhind Lectures at Edinburgh. My theme was 'The Origins of Insular Monasticism', and I cleared some ground by

---

5 Jonas, *Vita Sancti Columbani*, ed. B. Krusch (Hanover, 1905).

discussing Patrick, and his (late) dating, and his geographical area, and what he tells us about himself, in a very specific way; first and foremost, a classic example of a missionary. Not enough of us, involved with the study of early Christianity in these isles, tap into an extraordinarily rich and illuminating genre of literature – the memoirs, the dispatches home, the biographies of nineteenth-century missionaries, particularly those of the Church of Scotland and the evangelical movements, in remote regions of Africa, Asia and global extremities. They are notably illuminating when it comes to questions of how to disseminate the Gospels to illiterates confined to their own obscure vernaculars. The career of Patrick can be matched, in a great many details, by the figure I chose; Edmund J. Peck, who worked among the Eskimos around Hudson's Bay.[6]

What this also demonstrated (and I just summarize it here) is that in the half-century 450 to 500, a half-century that certainly included Patrick's death, the occurrence throughout Ireland of any sort of literacy, any use of a second language (Latin rather than British), any spin-off from Late Roman Britain, any knowledge of Christianity, was far from uniform. You can demonstrate this with the aid of archaeology, epigraphy and place-names. In the simplest way, there must clearly be significance in the overall distribution of stones incised with the ogam alphabet. Regardless of when ogam was invented (I believe quite possibly by AD 300),[7] where and by who (I believe, somewhere in the deep southwest, perhaps by a committee rather than an individual but if so a committee familiar with Latin) and why (I believe, to provide a monumental script for personal memorials imitating those of Late Roman Britain and Gaul, but avoiding Roman *capitalis* with nine curved letters out of twenty), it seems patent that this fashion barely touched the province, the ten or eleven subsequent counties, in which Patrick is most likely to have worked (fig. 1.1). We must also remember that, unlike his subsequent and partly-fictitious biographers, Patrick makes no mention whatsoever of Christian burial in his own day. Let us consider another map that I first showed in 1995 at the Munster conference (fig. 1.2). A minimum of six

---

6 Arthur Lewis, *The life and work of the Rev. E.J. Peck among the Eskimos* (London, 1904).
7 Charles Thomas, 'Early medieval Munster: thoughts upon its primary Christian phase', in M.A. Monk and J. Sheehan (eds), *Early medieval Munster: archaeology, history and society* (Cork, 1998), 10–11; Damian McManus, *A guide to ogam* (Maynooth, 1991), 29–30, 40–1.

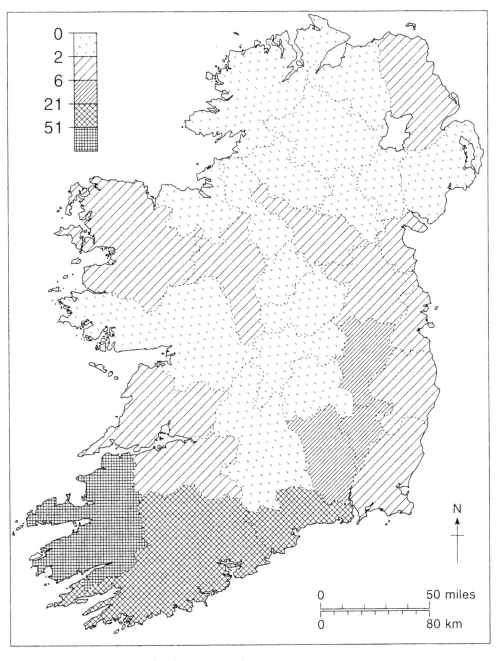

1.1 Density distribution map of ogam-inscribed memorial stones
© Charles Thomas 1998, by permission of Cork University Press

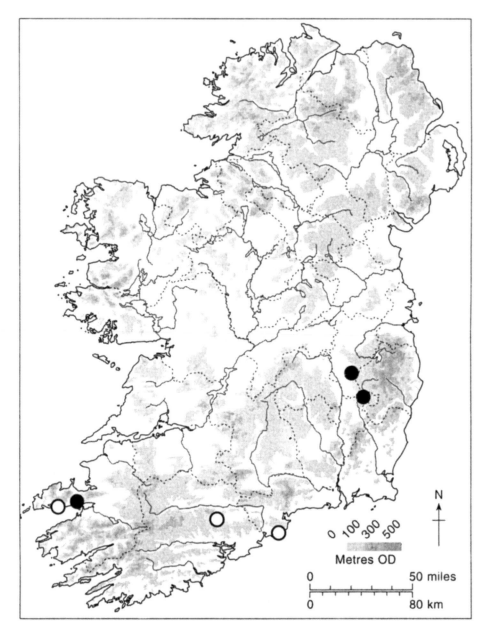

1.2 Distribution map of ogam memorials with Roman personal names:
● son's name Irish, father's Roman; ○ single Roman name.
© Charles Thomas 1998, by permission of Cork University Press

ogam stones exhibit in ogam, recognisable Roman names on their own – AMATUS, MARIANUS, SAGITTARIUS – and (three of them) father-and-son, where the *son's* name is Irish but the *father's* was Roman – as genitives, DUNAIDONAS son of MARIANUS, COIMAGNAS son of VITALINUS, and a MAQIDECCEDAS son of MARINUS. All are south of, four very much south of, a line across from Galway to Dublin.

I want to leave this, and further implications, aside for a moment, and return to two themes, the second of which ought to bring us back to Skerries and district. The accomplishments, the learning, the literary knowledge of Columbanus – one of the most important early Irish writers and scholars, though by no means alone – tell us that, somewhere in Leinster, by the middle of the sixth century, a clever lad from a well-off family could be taught Latin, effectively up to the third or *rhetoricus* level, get to know not just Jerome's Vulgate but other writings by Jerome, read Gildas' *De Excidio* not all that long after its publication in 540, and, either in his late teens, or, more certainly, after joining the monastery at Bangor, master an impressive further range of both patristic and secular Latin writings. Supposing that (at the very least) Latinity at this level was available in other parts of modern Leinster and Munster, how do we explain this? For fifth-sixth century Ireland, there are several ways (and that excludes appealing to any presence, in fourth-century Leinster and Munster, of Latin-speaking immigrants, traders or tax-exiles from Britannia). First, though popular literature and secondary histories have not always caught up with recent thinking, we must abandon the old notion that in the year AD 410, or 425, or whenever, the lights went out in Roman Britain, and a country with four million people was plunged overnight into the Dark Ages; its eastern half ravaged, with fire, pillage and rape, an irresistible red tide of pagan savagery consisting of, perhaps, ten thousand Germanic-speaking invaders. Well into the sixth century, at least two-thirds of what is now England, Wales and southern Scotland contained an ongoing Christianity, scattered adherences to romanitas, widespread use of Latin alongside the neo-Brittonic languages, and, at certain places, an educational system, a minority one, modelled on the fourth-century private schools of grammarians. People travelled around to attend these; mostly top people, and any such schools were mostly the preserve of the Church. Best-known, far-famed, was the late fifth-century school headed by Iltutus at Llantwit Fawr in the Glamorgan coastal plain, south-east Wales; based on a substantial 'gentleman's monastery' on Gaulish lines. Broadly contemporary pupils included Samson (of Dol), son of an aristocrat in north Pembrokeshire; the future king Maelgwn of Gwynedd, whose home was in Anglesey; and Gildas himself, from some other part of the country. The principal focus of this sub-Roman Latin culture was across much of south Wales, a region we can envisage as being in continuous contact, Fishguard to Rosslare, with south-east Ireland. It may be an accident of history that the Apostle of Ireland was himself an hundred-per-cent Briton, all the indications being that his homeland was the area beyond Carlisle. It is *no* accident of history that, initially, those parts of Britannia beyond the English conquests, certain of the post-500 native kingdoms, provided the cultural bridge between the high literary culture of fourth-century Britannia and the later levels of accomplishment in Ireland that we have seen exemplified by Columbanus.

The second element is external, maritime, contact. Whatever was happening in northern Gaul and the Rhineland frontier, however many pirates and freebooting raiders – Irish, Pictish, Jutish – roamed the northern seas, regular passages between southern and eastern Ireland, Wales and the south-west, and Atlantic France must have continued largely unabated.[8] We ought to think of vessels mainly on the scale of modern seagoing fishing boats. We ought also to remember that passage by sea, often unavoidable, was frequently slow and unpleasant – Constantius' Life of St Germanus tells us how bishops Germanus and Lupus, sailing in the 420s from Boulogne to somewhere like Folkestone, had such an appallingly rough crossing that poor old Lupus was able to describe it, in full and horrible detail, nearly fifty years afterwards.[9] Where possible, you hopped across the channels and then went overland to the next port (we'll return to this point later). The evidence for Insular-Gaulish contact from the fifth century onwards comes from various things. By 460–470 Christian memorials in western France were adopting the formulae HIC IACIT, HIC IN TUMULO IACIT ('here lies'; 'here in the tomb lies') and this is plainly

---

8 Charles Thomas, 'Gallici nautae de Galliarum Provinciis: a sixth/seventh century trade with Gaul reconsidered', *Medieval Archaeology*, 34 (1990), 1–26. **9** Constantius, *Vita Sancti Germani Autissiodorensis*, ed. W. Levison (Hanover, 1919).

the source for their appearance, before 500, in Cornwall and parts of Wales. And we have glimpses, important ones, of how cultural links were maintained and fed. Perhaps around 520, Samson (of Dol) found himself in the island monastery headed by Abbot Piro, an offshoot of Llantwit Fawr; Ynys Bŷr or Caldey Island, just off Tenby. Quite by chance, they were visited there by certain distinguished Irishmen, on their way from Rome – men who Samson found, in conversing with them, to be truly learned men, *phylosophi*. In this seventh-century Life, the episode is entirely incidental; the point is that any conversation would have been in Latin, and these Irishmen, who would land at Tenby and go across to somewhere like Cardigan for the final stage of return, had very probably just sailed across from north Cornwall. The reverse trip – Carmarthen Bay, to the Camel estuary by Padstow, then south overland to Fowey, then a second boat to Armorica – is what Samson himself undertook a few years later. Again, in the eleventh century Life of St Cadog (of Llancarfan), son of king Gwynllyw of Gwent, and grandson of king Brychan of Brycheiniog, Cadog is said to be coming home from three years' education in Ireland, at Lismore, Co. Waterford (we are now in the second half of the sixth century, which may be too early for Lismore, but never mind). He lands, perhaps at St David's, and travels east; but stops off in Brecon, his late grandfather's realm, because he hears that a *famosus rhetoricus*, a celebrated teacher at the highest level, *nuper de Italia advenisse*, had lately arrived there from Italy – for which read 'the Continent' – and Cadog wanted to be instructed by him Romano more Latinitate, in Latinity after the Roman style.[10] This man's name has been slightly mangled into Bachan or Pachan; he was real enough, was called Paschen, Pascentius, and was included by name as Paschent in a local mass roll dating to not much after 600, one of the earliest in Europe.

When we move into the seventh century, crude archaeology to some extent takes over, as with distribution-maps of the imported class of northern or Atlantic Gaulish pottery known as E ware (figs. 1.3, 1.4), probably accompanying less visible imports of wine in barrel.[11] In his *Life*, Jonas implies that Columbanus and friends, leaving Bangor around

---

10 Vita Sancti Cadoci, §11; A.W. Wade-Evans, *Vitae Sanctorum Britanniae et Genealogiae* (Cardiff, 1944), 48–9. 11 See note 8 above.

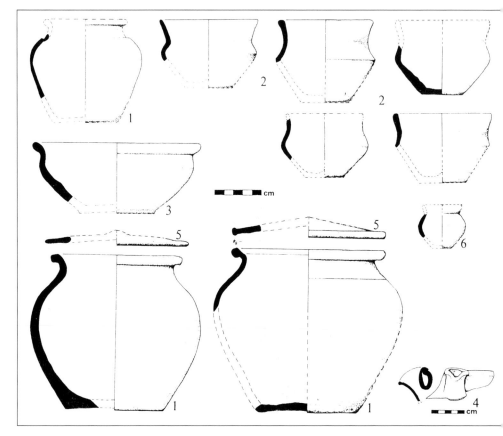

1.3 Imported pottery: examples of E-ware: drawings by Mary O'Donnell of Irish finds

590 and bound for France, travelled 'by way of the British shores'; if correct, across to Wales, then over and across Cornwall, perhaps (as elsewhere recorded) landing at St Riquier on the Normandy coast. On the other hand, when, in 610, Columbanus was involved in a particularly stormy episode in Burgundy, and, with his followers, was about to be banished, he sailed down the Loire to Nantes, where local dignitaries were ordered to place him on a trading-ship, said to be bound directly for Ireland (stormy weather saved the day, and the exile was avoided).

If you were important, and rich, you could probably hire a vessel; like Samson, who sailed across to Cornwall in a boat large enough to hold him, his father Ammon, his cousin Enoc, possibly twenty others,

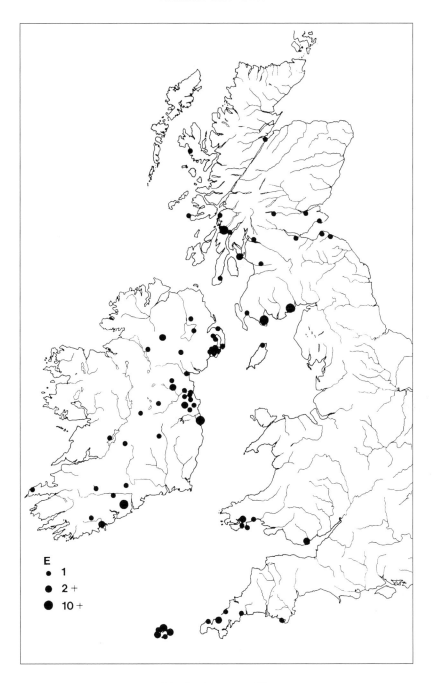

1.4 Distribution map of E-ware

enough baggage to fill a wagon, and his own light two-wheeled *currus*. Having landed, he simply sent the ship away.[12] If poor and on the run, like the youthful St Patrick, you reached the shore and hung around, until some boat, bound for anywhere, agreed to take you along. We are now going to deal with someone who was important, would have been in a position to obtain a crossing on demand, and may very well have landed hereabouts; we know who he was, and why he came, and when, and, despite the best efforts of the hegemony-seeking, later seventh-century, Church of Armagh, I aim to tell you a good deal about him. Our starting point is what Columbanus wrote to his pulverised pope in 613 – 'the Faith – as it was delivered by you first'.

Prosper of Aquitaine, a cultured Christian layman, was born around 390 and when young lived in Marseilles, where he became swept up into the exciting and challenging new world of monastic endeavours there. He also became a fervent champion, against the heresies of Pelagius, of St Augustine's teachings about Grace and free will. In 430 he went to Rome, met Pope Celestine the First, and urged him to write to the bishops of Gaul condemning anti-Augustinian views. Then he returned for a while to Marseilles, where he wrote, among other things, an *Epitome Chronicae*, a potted world history to AD 433 (this was a special interest of his). Finally he went back again to Rome, entered the service of Pope Leo I as a *notarius* and, having updated his Chronicle to AD 455, died in that year.

In 429, Prosper noted that heresy was present in Britain as well as Gaul. Specifically a Pelagian heretic Agricola, son of a Pelagian bishop Severianus, was insidiously corrupting the congregations of Britain, *ecclesias Britanniae*, with his teachings; this suggests that the unknown Agricola, wherever he operated, was influential. But, through the negotiation of the deacon Palladius, Pope Celestine sent Germanus bishop of Auxerre to act on his behalf; and Germanus routed these heretics and directed the Britons to the Catholic Faith.

Under the year 431 Prosper again mentions Palladius, whom he must have known personally; of a notable *gens*, either a personal deacon to

---

12 The episode is analyzed in Charles Thomas, *And shall these mute stones speak? Post-Roman inscriptions in Western Britain* (Cardiff, 1994), chap. 14, with further references.

bishop Germanus at Auxerre, or acting as a papal deacon. 'Palladius was ordained by pope Celestine, and sent to the Irish believers in Christ' (*ad Scotos, in Christum credentes*) 'as the first bishop'.[13] Why? We get the answer in cap. 21 of Prosper's short tract *Liber contra collatorem* (a riposte to John Cassian, who had dared to question St Augustine's stand on grace and free will). Listing steps taken by successive popes to defend orthodoxy, and to assert papal primacy in outlying provinces of the empire, Prosper spells out the actions of Celestine, pope from 422 to 432, including these several Insular interventions:

> And with no less active a concern, he freed Britain from the same disease (i.e., Pelagian heresy)
> when he shut out, from their remote Ocean retreat, certain enemies of grace who were in possession of their ancestral lands (this is the 429 visit by Germanus and Lupus)
> and, ordaining a bishop for the Irish, he made the barbarian island Christian, while taking care to keep the Roman Island Catholic (i.e. to keep Britain orthodox).[14]

There you have it, as clear as daylight. The statement that in AD 431, absolute date, Celestine despatched Palladius as *primus episcopus, ad Scotos in Christum credentes*, is the single most important external reference in Ireland's history. Building on the earlier undated introduction of some element of Latin literacy, it marks Ireland's tardy incorporation into Europe; and it sheds more light on Irish Christian beginnings than all of St Patrick's writings. It also provides a starting-point for Irish monasticism. And in the morass, manoeuvring, and muddles, of the next 250 years within Irish Christian records, Prosper's little chronicle-entry could not be set aside, and it was not forgotten; despite the later Armagh drive to render Palladius a kind of Orwellian non-person.

It is a truism among historians, and I suppose it remains the favourite argument for a 'late' Patrick, that revisionists at the alleged proto-Patrician foundation, the episcopal church of Armagh, faced with this immutable record of what happened in 431 were stuck, and knew they

---

13 Liam de Paor, *St Patrick's world* (Dublin, 1993), translation, 79. **14** Ibid., 71.

were stuck, with 432 as the earliest credible date for Patrick's return to Ireland as a bishop – a *second* bishop. The hard pill could be mollified by having Palladius fail dismally, or die, or quit in despair for Pictland as soon as possible. Further awkwardness arose, probably by the seventh century, from the annalistic date of 493 for the death of Patrick; and worse, a date of 535 (or 103 years on from 432) for the death of an acceptably historic Mochta or Maucteus,[15] said to have been Patrick's younger disciple, a Briton whose existence was still known to Adomnán of Iona in the 680s.

The reason that we cannot turn at once to modern critical editions of any *Vita Palladii, Acta Palladii, Dicta Palladii,* is not that none of them ever existed. They did, and quite a few people knew of them. It is that by the early eighth century, almost without exception, all and any records of Palladius had been misappropriated to St Patrick, bypassing a slight obstacle that Patrick's writings make no reference to any other named evangelist. The monolithic claim of the post-Patrick church of Armagh is fancifully set out in the mid-seventh century tract *Liber Angeli.* In imitation of the *Confessio,* Patrick is made to undergo yet another angelic dream visitation. The angel assures him (and all intended readers) that Armagh merits a *terminus vastissimus,* a *paruchia,* embracing the whole of Ireland, a spiritual overlordship that reflects Patrick's missionary labours.[16] But here, from whatever tangled background, is a mind-set, that must have known – in writing – far more about Palladius than we ever can today; knew that Prosper's uncompromising record of a 431 arrival was beyond challenge; but was on course to reduce the Leinster landing of Palladius with his companions to the intrusion of a funny foreigner, who dithered ineffectually for a bit, and then died, or departed. You can indeed fool most people for a very long time.

Let us, however, go back to those three short extracts from Prosper, and spell out their inferences. The Scoti, believing in Christ, were Christians in Ireland, generally the barbarian island because it was outside the Imperial *limites,* but that does not mean they all had to be exclusively Irish natives. They had no previous bishop (and, *per* Professor

---

15 *AU* 493, 535. 16 Liber Angeli; Ludwig Bieler, *The Patrician texts in the Book of Armagh* (Dublin, 1979), 185.

Dan Binchy, as yet no loanword from *episcopus*). But, as Christian group-ings, *ecclesiae*, they were, in 431, numerous enough, or spatially con-centrated enough, or both, to warrant a first bishop. It is then likely that a Christian presence went back some decades; at a diffused scale, those believers could have had some rudimentary churches already and some officiating priests, perhaps later elevated in memory as those obscure pre-Patrician saints. We can certainly assume worship and instruction took place in Latin, using pre-Vulgate Biblical texts; and that goes along with a previously-conveyed picture of Latinity in Ireland by, and considerably before, the year 400. Their first bishop, Palladius, was not a provincial chosen for them by a British synod. He was a man of standing, influ-entially connected, a papal favourite chosen for the job, and he had already been prominent (as Prosper knew) in a campaign to combat the Pelagian heresy threatening Britain. *Ergo*, Rome had perceived a danger of heretical infection reaching the Christian innocents of *Hiberione*, which argues for repeated Irish-British contact (west Wales to Leinster and south-east Munster, say), and a measure of correspondence, if not also official visits, to arrange a suitable reception for Bishop Palladius. But do not picture Palladius wading ashore wherever it was, a lonely figure, with a grip in his hand, slithering among seaweed. Germanus and Lupus were supported by a regular throng of their Gaulish followers. We shall identify likely members of Palladius' *familia*; and make a good guess as to at least part of his *volumina atque impedimenta*.

The post-1940 literature about the Palladius-Patrick question, or conflation of the two separate bishops, is extensive if not acrimonious. It has concerned me only insofar as I have believed for years that the real Patrick, a man deservedly to be admired and a man whom I presented to you earlier as a most notable missionary can be found, and can only be found, in what he himself wrote. Reading what Ludwig Bieler brought together as 'The Patrician Texts in the Book of Armagh', the truth struck me as so glaringly obvious that, where the bulk of the commentaries by learned Jesuits and the modern Patrician expansionists are on offer, I have read them all with a detached sense of a visit to Disneyland.

One by-product of Armagh's drive to establish, historically-justifiable, hegemony over the entire realm of Ireland's Christianity was an invention, in the seventh century, of a doublet. The concept of a Patrick,

Apostle to the Irish, was divided like an amoeba. It was claimed that the 431 Palladius was really, or also, called Patricius (*qui Patricius alio nomine appellabatur*), whence a distinction became neccessary between an 'Old Patrick', *senex Patricius*, Sen-Phatric, or Palladius; and a younger, later one, *Patricius secundus*, Patrick the Briton, who died 493. The more readily then could all and any of the doings, remembered sayings, written references, and associated *dramatis personae* of Palladius – *senex Patricius* – be transferred to the inflated Patrick of what some have called 'the Armagh propagandists'.

We see this in the *Vita Sancti Patricii*, the Life, by Muirchú, composed about 690, and largely couched as an historical narrative. Briefly paraphrasing Patrick's own account of his childhood and youth, up to his escape from Ireland (aged 22) in someone's ship, Muirchú has to mention Palladius: 'For they were well aware that Palladius, archdeacon of Pope Celestine, had been consecrated and sent to convert this island' – but Palladius was ill-received, set out to return home and died in the land of the British.[17] Meanwhile, Patrick has been four years in Gaul, with Germanus in Auxerre; having received the visionary call to return to the Irish, he is about to be sent there by Germanus, along with an older priest Segitius, when news comes of Palladius' death. Patrick then turns to a very important bishop called Amathorex, who conferred upon him the episcopal grade, and ordained Patrick's companions Auxilius and Iserninus (these two names are important) and some others. The party boards a ship, arrives in Britain and then, speedily and with a favourable wind, sailed across *mare nostrum* to Ireland. The rest of Muirchú consists of Irish adventures, King Lóegaire, Tara and the first Easter, the foundation of Armagh; things none of which is found in Patrick's writings, and which need not bother us.

It is in the *Collectanea*, the so-called Memoir of Tírechán, regarded as slightly earlier than Muirchú's Life – about 670 – that the partly-planned mythologizing takes off. Tírechán, a bishop, had been pupil of Bishop Ultán of Connor; he had read material in a book that Ultán possessed. His summary of the early part of the *Confessio* is even shorter than Muirchú's and, after Patrick's escape from Ireland aged 22:

---

17 Muirchú, 'Vita Sancti Patricii'; Bieler, *Patrician texts*, 61.

Seven other years he walked, and sailed on water, in plains, and in mountain valleys, throughout Gaul, and the whole of Italy, and the islands in the Tyrrhene sea (that is, the triangle surrounded by Sardinia, Sicily and southern Italy): as he himself said in an account of his labours. In one of these islands, which is called *Aralanensis*, he stayed for 30 years, as bishop Ultan testified to me.

Patrick came with his Gauls (*cum Gallis*) to the islands of Mochu Chor and the eastern island which is called Patrick's island (this appears to contain an early Leinster tradition) and with him there was a great number of holy bishops and priests and deacons and exorcists and janitors (*ostiarii*) and lectors, let alone the sons (or young men; *filii*) that he had ordained.[18]

We are given, in the Book of Armagh collection that contains this earlier Memoir, a great long list of the names of all these people, one section of which is headed 'On the names of the Franks of Patrick'; and in someone's supplementary notes, a very precise statement:

> In the thirteenth year of the emperor Theodosius, bishop Patricius is sent by bishop Celestine, pope of Rome, for the teaching of the Scots.[19]

Notice the Imperial, though not also western Consular, dating; this comes ultimately from Prosper's Chronicle, in which year 430–1 is headed 'Theodosio XIII, tredecimo'. Then we have: 'Bishop Palladius is sent first', *Palladius episcopus primo mittitur* (here Prosper has *Palladius, et primus episcopus mittitur*) 'who was named *Patricius* with another name, who suffered martyrdom at the hands of the Scots'. Next, this particular Armagh writer redresses the imbalance: 'Then Patricius is sent second by the angel Victor and Pope Celestine; – he was believed by all Ireland and baptised almost all of it.'

Finally, there are four short 'sayings of Patrick', only two of which need engage our attention (and if Patrick the Briton ever uttered any one of them, I will personally be Joan of Arc);

---

18 Tírechán, 'Collectanea'; Bieler, *Patrician texts*, 125–7. **19** Additamenta to the Book of Armagh; Bieler, *Patrician texts*, 129, 165.

The fear of God I had as my guide through the Gauls (*per Gallias*) and Italy, and the islands which are in the Tyrrhene sea.

Church of the Irish (*aeclessia Scotorum*), nay of the Romans, in order that you be Christians, as are the Romans, you must sing at every hour of prayer that praiseworthy utterance, *Kyrie eleison, Christe eleison*; let each and every Christian flock that makes up my following (*omnis aeclessia quae sequitur me*) sing Kyrie eleison, Christe eleison, Deo gratias.[20]

I am not going to lead you further through this minefield, in which too many academic limbs have already been maimed or blown off. These are remnants, having percolated north from at least one centre in Leinster to Armagh and probably other Ulster churches, of the *acta*, the contemporary records, and a few numbered sayings, of Palladius. Actually there is a lot of valuable historical detail here. Remembering that Palladius was in the first place chosen, consecrated and sent under the twin aegis of Pope Celestine and Bishop Germanus it would be quite incredible that he and his companions would not have sent reports of progress, success, safeguarding against heresy, back to base: back to Auxerre, if not also Rome, to Celestine and Leo.

There were written sources; probably at Auxerre, *Autissiodunum*. There is a give-away line in Tírechán's Memoir, possibly taken from whatever book of Ultán's he had consulted and in a relation to a chronology of one hundred and eleven years of Patrick's life:

Haec Constans in Gallis invénit.
(These things, Constans discovered in Gaul.)[21]

Some Irish cleric in the earlier seventh century had been able to read, and presumably to make notes and copy out lists of proper names from, the Palladian dispatches.

For a century at least, there have been those – great men, good men (like dear Ludwig Bieler) among them – who in the extra details

20 Ibid., 125.   **21** Tírechán, 'Collectanea'; Bieler, *Patrician texts*, 123.

provided by Muirchú, Tírechán and the Armagh *additimenta* have chosen to see, have wanted to see, evidence of a Patrick who may, veritably, have gone as far as Rome; was indeed ordained or consecrated by Germanus, or his predecessor-bishop, at Auxerre, Amator; and spent a period on the island monastery of *Lerina*, Lérins. But none of this stands. Lerina is by no stretch of geography in the Tyrrhenian sea; these islands lie just off Cannes, and Lerina, Ile Saint-Honorat, site of Honoratus' early fifth-century foundation, still contains a monastery. In any event Tírechán's statement that 'in an account of his labours', *in commemoratione laborum*, which bishop Ultán apparently possessed, Patrick 'stayed for 30 years in one of these islands which is called Aralensis' has nothing to do with Lerina, or Patrick. This is a shorter episode in the life of Palladius; for Aralensis read *Arelatensis*, or *Arelatense civitas*: the ancient city of Arles. Hilary, a nobleman, had been converted to the ascetic life by St Honoratus and around 420 taken to the monastery at Lerina; then he followed Honoratus to Arles when his mentor became bishop there, and was himself elected the next bishop in 430–1. This is a wholly persuasive setting for any short but impressionable stay by a contemporary Palladius; a man who did most certainly travel throughout Gaul and Italy before his Irish prelacy.

When in 431 Palladius arrived to oversee the *credentes* of Leinster, I (for one) believe that he brought not only sufficient companions in appropriate clerical orders to set up a papally-approved diocese, or more than one diocese; but also a large selection of the kind of literature one would expect, including the available range – by 430, quite extensive – of monastic books, Desert Fathers' work, histories, collections, rules. Palladius, unusually as a named person in a known year, stands for Ireland's monastic origins. We recall why he had been sent; to make the barbarian Ireland Christian but also to prevent heretical infection from Christian Britain. In that second of the Dicta Patricii (*recte*, Dicta *Palladii*) 'in order that you be Christians as are the Romans' may imply a little more. Does it mean 'orthodox Christians, as are the Romans', a state to be ensured by following their new bishop's teaching in every respect?

If Palladius worked in Ireland for, say, twenty to thirty years, gradually extending his initial, East Leinster, episcopate to further notional dioceses under additional bishops in southern Leinster and most of

Munster, does absolutely no trace of this survive? What Tírechán's Bishop Ultán had in a book, which the mysterious Constans found somewhere in Gaul, apparently dealt only with Palladius' Gaulish-Italian background, Auxerre, Amator and Germanus, and perhaps reports from the spiritual front line. But we do have a very strange document indeed; called variously 'The Synod of the Bishops' and 'The First Synod of Saint Patrick'. To dissect it backwards, the sole manuscript (CCC 279 or 0.20, *ex* Worcester Cathedral) was ascribed, by Bischoff, to the later ninth century, written on the Continent, perhaps near Tours. If so, it was a faithful copy, reproducing the Insular GRA of *gratias*, of an Irish exemplar that, one would guess, came from the Armagh area in the later seventh. That, in its turn, was an enlarged and somewhat re-arranged version – also faithfully copying a few selective contractions – from a genuine fifth-century original. It starts with:

> Here begins the synod of the bishops (*episcoporum*), that is of Patricius, Auxilius, Isserninus. We give thanks to God the Father and the Son and the Holy Spirit. To the priests and deacons and every cleric, the bishops Patricius, Auxilius and Isserninus, greetings.[22]

There follow thirty-four rulings, or provisions, or canons, plainly out of order – out of five logical groupings – and some probably of secondary insertion.

Ludwig Bieler persisted in arguing that this was genuinely a product from the real Patrick, the Briton, and even produced a date of 457 by emending an annalistic year. Binchy, on the strength of several canons dealing with native Irish legal points, and his reading of wording in others, thought it a wholly native product of the mid-seventh century reflecting the Romanizing versus native parties' controversy on the date of Easter and related disputes. Kathleen Hughes offered a compromise of the mid-sixth century. And I think that likely – a very early *Leinster*

---

22 Ludwig Bieler and Daniel Binchy, *The Irish penitentials* (Dublin, 1963), 54–9, 184–97; David N. Dumville, *Councils and synods of the Gaelic early and central Middle Ages*, Quiggin Pamphlets on the Sources of Medieval Gaelic History, no. 3 (Cambridge, 1997), 6–17; M.J. Faris (ed.), *The Bishops' Synod ('The First Synod of St Patrick'): a symposium with text, translation and commentary*, ARCA 1, Dept. Classics, University of Liverpool (Liverpool, 1976).

copy of the original, ending up at Armagh, where 'PALLADIUS' was altered to 'PATRICIUS', perhaps just a palimpsest, scraping out the middle four letters LLAD and writing in TRIC (both names, nine letters, start PA and end IUS).

I believe we have here an ecclesiastic governance, for a part of Ireland, issued possibly fifteen or twenty years on from 431 by Palladius and two others – Auxilius, Iserninus – who were, by then, bishops of new dioceses. It is the words used that lead me to that conclusion (and a certainty that this has nothing whatsoever to do with Patrick). One could pick out, as fifth-century Gaulish Latin and possibly southern British Latin – but not taken into Irish usage – *plebs* to mean what we would now call 'a parish'; *aecclesia* for both 'the Church' (an abstract word) and 'a church as a building', where for canon 24, *aecclesiam* (*aedificet*), my guess is that Patrick would have written *dominicum*; a distinction, talking about bishops, between *episcopus*, a bishop in an administrative guise, but *sacerdos* as to his priestly function; and then we have canon 33, one of a group governing the status of intrusive or of wandering clerics (*vagus, vagulus*). 'A cleric whom comes to us from the Britains without a letter, although he may be resident in a parish (*in plebe*), is not permitted to minister.' 'From the Britains' is *de Britanis*, geographical plural, in the fourth–early fifth century, suggesting the four (or five) *provinciae* of Britannia (single). This, with perhaps two more canons, takes us back to Palladius as Prosper shows him; the papally-authorized custodian of orthodoxy, and these are precautions against would-be Pelagians drifting across from Britannia.

Whether in this document the references to *monachus et virgo*, not allowed to stay in the same *hospitium* nor travel nor talk together, or to punishment of a monk who wanders without consulting his abbot, could be primary, or more likely from the seventh century, I am not sure. The picture one gets – from these few sources, but also from the better-evidenced European setting of *primus episcopus* Palladius – is a 431 venture, sponsored by Rome *via* Auxerre, trying to implant an orthodox Continental church hierarchy in a part of Ireland that – for reasons we looked at earlier – was ready to take that on board; but, incidentally, as a by-product, also introducing monastic models conveyed in literature that found an equally receptive Christian populace.

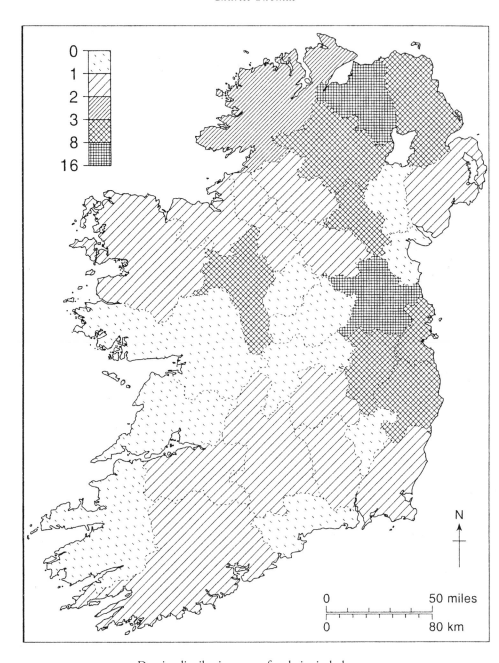

1.5 Density distribution map of ecclesiastical placenames
prefixed with the element *Domnach*
© Charles Thomas 1998, by permission of Cork University Press

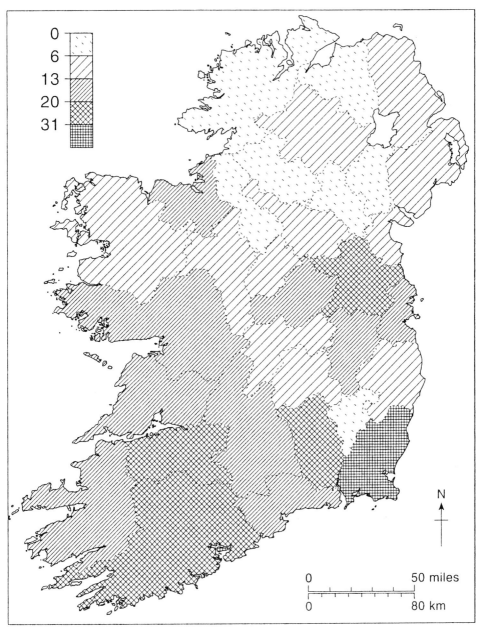

1.6 Density distribution map of ecclesiastical placenames
prefixed with the element *Cell*
© Charles Thomas 1998, by permission of Cork University Press

Before concluding, I don't propose to go into a long and detailed digression about place-name evidence, which anyhow is in print elsewhere, but I wish to consider two more maps to emphasize the different backgrounds of the Patrician north, and the larger southerly Palladian part of Ireland. The prefix Donagh (as Donaghmore, Donaghadee) comes from an extremely early word, British Latin *Dominicum*, Primitive Irish *Dominech*, then *Domnach*, 'a Christian church building'. The northern focus is the area of Patrick's missionary decades and their aftermath; the Leinster one, where the pre-431 *credentes*, Irish believers in Christ, surely an implant from fourth-century Romano-British Christianity, were to be found (fig. 1.5). Contrast the distributional weight with the next one, place-names formed originally, with another loanword, Primitive and Old Irish *cell*, rather than *cill* (fig. 1.6). This is a purely literary borrowing, by those understanding Latin, from *cella* 'Christian locality, of eremitic or monastic nature' (and subsequently a wider range of meanings). The source was entirely literary. Patrick did not know and could never have possessed the literature in question, which is identifiable; Palladius and his *familia* would have known it, and are more than likely to have introduced and diffused it. The map repeats that Palladian, Leinster, focus and then the adoption predominantly to the south and west. T.F. O'Rahilly wrote of 'The Two Patricks'. In turn, I myself do not, but could, write of 'Two Christian Irelands' before the sixth century; the Patrician North, and a Leinster-Munster south. The explanation partly appears in the previous ogam map. The south was the area with the much greater, the essential, penetration of a knowledge of the Latin language. It was the seed-bed for subsequent monasticism; and the eclipsed Palladius was the agent.

Finally, the $64,000 question, with the answer that must follow if one is able to recognize the misprisions of the Armagh propagandists. Palladius cannot, alas, come across to us in the same intensely human guise as Patrick, but he deserves a better treatment than footnotes. Starting out in 431 with his retinue, he could have gone north and down the Seine, or west to the Loire, to find a ship; in either case, the Channel crossing to south west Britain, then overland, perhaps saw the party in south-west Wales. The journey would have taken some weeks. A Leinster-coast arrival is strongly indicated; there is, of course, a tradition that it was at the estuarine, boat-building Wicklow port of Arklow (Bowen rightly pointed out that this, at any rate, suggests a final crossing from Cardigan Bay).[23] In some fashion this must have arisen from the claim in Muirchú's Life of Patrick that Patrick landed 'in portum ... Hostium Dee' – Inver Dee, immediately below modern Arklow. It would be improbably far south for Patrick at any stage. But we have been told; in the slightly earlier Memoir by Tírechán, the man who made such good use of what Ultán had in writing, what Constans had found in Gaul, which really concerned the life and *acta* of Palladius. 'Patrick came with his Gauls to the islands of Moccu Chor, and to the eastern island which is called Patrick's island.' Yes, but for how long had the latter been so re-named? and by whom, and in whose interests? Behind this must lie a purely Leinster, non-Armagh, non-Patrician attribution at least as early as the sixth century. The person who came 'with his Gauls', whose Irish landfall was your offshore isles (where indeed the party may cautiously have camped for a while), was Palladius. That makes Skerries the point where, in AD 431, partly-Christian Ireland was joined to largely-Christian Europe. You are entitled to celebrate this. In the remaining lectures, my colleagues will be more concerned with later Patrician themes, in which Palladius has little part; but I share with you a conviction that this conference is in the right place, and at the right time.

---

23 E.C. Bowen, *Saints, seaways and settlements in the Celtic lands* (Cardiff, 1969), 121–4.

Medieval sub-kingdoms of Brega: the kingships of Calatruim, Déssi Breg, Mugdornae Breg and Uí Maic Uais Breg

EDEL BHREATHNACH

Dominance over the midland and eastern over-kingdoms of Brega and Mide by Uí Néill dynasties is strongly reflected in the sources and in its wake has led to the overshadowing, and in some cases expunging, of the sub-kingdoms and dynasties of the region. Evidence relating to those which were over-shadowed survives sporadically in the annals, in genealogies and in other sources including hagiography and martyrologies. Occasionally they have been commented on by scholars when dealing with the vicissitudes of Uí Néill kingdoms or with particularly important sites in the region.[1] This paper seeks to advance the knowledge regarding a number of these smaller kingdoms by building a profile of their kings, the structure of their kingships and the extent of their territories, insofar as they can be reconstructed.

OCCASIONAL KINGSHIPS

The inclusion of a place-name, and particularly a prehistoric monument or royal residence, in a royal title is a common occurrence throughout medieval Ireland. Some provincial kingships were recognised by the use

---

1 For the most comprehensive picture of the kingdoms and sub-kingdoms of Brega and Mide, see Paul Walsh, 'Meath in the Book of Rights' in John Ryan (ed.), *Féil-sgríbhinn Eóin Mhic Néill: essays and studies presented to Professor Eoin MacNeill* (Dublin 1940; reprint 1995), 508–21. For other important studies, see Francis John Byrne, 'Historical note on Cnogba (Knowth)' appendix to G. Eogan, 'Excavations at Knowth, Co. Meath, 1962–1965', *RIA Proc.*, 66C (1967–8), 383–400; Catherine Swift, '*Óenach Tailten*, the Blackwater Valley and the Uí Néill kings of Tara' in Alfred P. Smyth (ed.), *Seanchas. Studies in early and medieval Irish archaeology, history and literature in honour of Francis J. Byrne* (Dublin, 2000), 109–20; Paul Byrne, 'Ciannachta Breg before Síl nÁeda Sláine' in Smyth, ibid., 121–6; Michael Byrnes, 'The Árd Ciannachta in Adomnán's *Vita Columbae*: a reflection of Iona's attitude to the Síl nÁeda Sláine in the late seventh century', in Smyth, ibid., 127–36.

of the province's capital in the title, the most obvious being Cashel. Other titles could vary between a formula of RÍ/ REX + KINGDOM or RÍ/ REX + SITE. In Brega this formula is used in the alternation of the titles *rí/ rex deiscert Breg, rí/ rex Locha Gabor* (Lagore, Co. Meath) and *lethrí Breg* between the eighth and tenth centuries. In virtually all cases, however, the title *rí/ rex Locha Gabor* is accorded to the decendants of Fergus mac Fogartaich meic Néill (d. 724) whose caput was at Lagore and Dunshaughlin.² Similar formulae less frequently used are those of *rí/ rex Cnogba* (Knowth, Co. Meath) or *rí/ rex Rátho Airthir* (Oristown, Co. Meath). The latter is accorded twice as a title in the ninth century to Cathal mac Fiachrach (d. 810) and his grandson Cernachán mac Cumascaigh (d. 866), descendants of Áed mac Dlúthaig (d. 701). Since Cathal is also accorded the title *rex uirorum Cúl* (*AU*) 'king of Fir Cúl', it appears that his dynasty sought to control the kingdom of north-west Brega and in attempting to do so either physically or symbolically sought to control its caput at Ráith Airthir.³ The title *rí/ rex Cnogba* occurs sporadically, and far less frequently than *rí/ rex Locha Gabor*, from the eighth to the tenth century. It would seem to have been used as an alternative for the title of the over-kingship of Breg (*rí/ rex Brega*). It may also be significant that Congalach (d. 956) mac Máele-mithig, king of Brega, was accorded the epithet Congalach Cnogba ('of Knowth'). There may have been a deliberate ploy in countering the claims of the dynasty of Cellach mac Flannacáin (d. 895), Máel-mithig's brother, to the over-kingship of Brega. Whereas Lagore and Ráith Airthir can be clearly classified as habitation sites, one a crannóg used primarily from the seventh to the tenth centuries (medieval phase),⁴ the other a ringfort of unknown date, Knowth was a different site and was probably viewed as possessing a different fascination to medieval kings. As a prehistoric monument of similar status to other tombs in the Boyne Valley or at Lough Crew, Knowth was inhabited by the dead and by otherworldly beings. Despite that, it seems that the tombs at Knowth were occupied

---

2 Byrne, 'Cnogba', table 2; Edel Bhreathnach, 'Authority and supremacy in Tara and its hinterland *c.*950–1200', *Discovery Programme Reports* 5 (1999), 1–23: 2–5; Bart Jaski, *Early Irish kingship and succession* (Dublin, 2000), 307 (Table 6). 3 Swift, '*Óenach Tailten*', 112–13. In this regard, it may have been no co-incidence that Cathal's grandson Cernachán was killed by a certain Móracán mac Áedacáin in 866. 4 Hugh O'Neill Hencken, 'Lagore crannóg. An Irish royal residence of the seventh to tenth centuries AD', *RIA Proc.*, 53 C (1950), 1–247.

during two main phases in the early medieval period, evidence existing for a ditched enclosure dating to about the eighth century and an open settlement principally dating to the tenth and eleventh centuries.[5] The earlier phase could signify the use of the site for ceremonial purposes only, coinciding perhaps with the first appearance of the title 'king of Knowth' in the annals (*AU* 789). The second phase, however, is more significant in that a dynasty seems to have erected a royal residence at Knowth and to have spent at least some seasons inhabiting what they must have known to be a tomb, considering that it had been plundered by the Vikings in the ninth century. Its use as a site of kingship may be compared with the great Scandinavian complex of Gamla Uppsala in Sweden, dominated by several large mounds and known as a religious cult centre.[6]

THE KINGSHIP OF CALATRUIM

A further feature of the formula RÍ/ REX + SITE is its occurrence in relation to one reign. *AU* 842[7] records that Máel-dúin mac Conaill, *rí Calatroma*, was captured by the Vikings (*geinnti*). His death at the hands of the Leinstermen in 846 is also recorded (*AU*).[8] Calatruim (Galtrim, barony of Lower Deece, Co. Meath) lies to the west of Dunshaughlin and Lagore. It is rarely mentioned in medieval sources. The *Fragmentary Annals of Ireland* relates that Blathmac and Diarmait sons of Áed Sláine died of plague in Calatruim and locate it in the old territory of Búaigne.[9] That it was the site of a royal fort is suggested by an incident in 777 (*AU*) in which a skirmish occurred between two of the grandsons of Cernach Sotal, Niall mac Conaill Grant (d. 778) and Cummascach mac Fogartaig (d. 797). Echtgus mac Buith, king of Déssi Breg and many others were killed *hi faitchi Caladroma* 'on the green of Calatruim'. The gathering

---

5 George Eogan, 'Life and living at Lagore', in Smyth, *Seanchas*, 64–82: 82.   **6** Else Roesdahl, *The Vikings* (London, 1991), 68, 70, 153.   **7** Also recorded in *AFM, Chron. Scot.* For a recent detailed survey of midland and northern Uí Néill kingships, see T.M. Charles-Edwards, 'The Uí Néill 695–743: the rise and fall of dynasties', *Peritia*, 16 (2002), 396–418. Charles-Edwards comments specifically on the kingships under consideration here (405) and suggests that 'these appear from the second half of the eighth century because the annals were being composed in Brega and also because they were by then prepared to notice titles of a lower rank....'   **8** Also recorded in *AFM, Chron. Scot.*   **9** Joan Newlon Radner (ed.), *Fragmentary Annals of Ireland* (Dublin, 1978), 14 (para. 28), 186–7. The element Búaigne survives in the place-name Dún Búaigne (Dunboyne, Co. Meath).

---

of a crowd in the *faitche* of Calatruim implies that an assembly was being held there, perhaps the proclamation of one or other of the protagonists (Niall and Cummascach) as king of southern Brega since both held that title for a time. The participation of Echtgus mac Buith, king of the most important old client people (*sen-chenéla* or *déssi*) of the region also points in the direction of the proclamation or inauguration of a king since one of the residual functions of the *déssi* was to approve the claimant to a kingship.[10] It is evident that Niall emerged victorious from the battle at Calatruim, since he is accorded the title *rí/ rex Locha Gabor* on his death in 778, but that his descendants did not hold onto the kingship. He may have started his attempt to usurp the kingship of southern Brega and to proclaim himself king at his royal residence – Calatruim – directly in opposition to those kings who were seated not far away at Lagore. This action resembles that of Máel-mithig mac Flannacáin's possible usurpation of the title *rí Brega* by establishing a dynasty and a royal title at Knowth. It also explains the next series of entries relating to Calatruim which deal with the reign of Máel-dúin mac Conaill. Máel-dúin is most likely to have been Niall's grandson, whose father Conall (d. 815) and uncle Diarmait (d. 826) were accorded the title *rí deiscirt Breg*. The title seems to have alternated at this period between what might be termed 'the Lagore dynasty' (descendants of Fogartach mac Néill) and 'the Calatruim dynasty' (descendants of Conall Grant mac Néill), as illustrated by the following tables:

Table 2.1 The Calatruim dynasty

Conall Grant (d. 718)
|
Niall (d. 778)
Rí Deiscirt Breg
|
Conall (d. 815)　　　　**Diarmait** (d. 826)
Rí Deiscirt Breg　　　　　Rí Deiscirt Breg
|
Máel-dúin (d. 846)
Rí Calatruim

10 *Bethu Phátraic: the Tripartite Life of Patrick*, ed. Kathleen Mulchrone (Dublin and London, 1939), 79–80. I wish to thank Thomas Charles-Edwards for drawing this reference to my attention.

Table 2.2 The Lagore dynasty

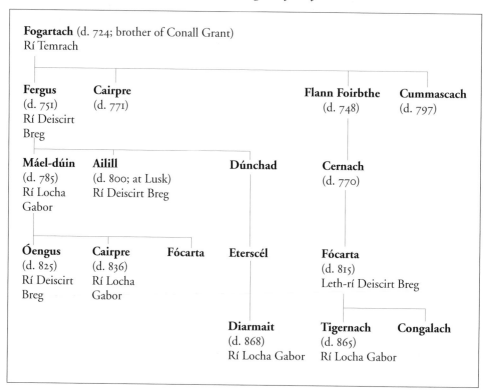

Fogartach (d. 724; brother of Conall Grant)
Rí Temrach

Fergus (d. 751) Rí Deiscirt Breg — **Cairpre** (d. 771) — **Flann Foirbthe** (d. 748) — **Cummascach** (d. 797)

Máel-dúin (d. 785) Rí Locha Gabor — **Ailill** (d. 800; at Lusk) Rí Deiscirt Breg — **Dúnchad** — **Cernach** (d. 770)

Óengus (d. 825) Rí Deiscirt Breg — **Cairpre** (d. 836) Rí Locha Gabor — **Fócarta** — **Eterscél** — **Fócarta** (d. 815) Leth-rí Deiscirt Breg

Diarmait (d. 868) Rí Locha Gabor — **Tigernach** (d. 865) Rí Locha Gabor — **Congalach**

Tigernach mac Focartai (d. 865) seems to have been a particularly active king, a factor which may have affected Máel-dúin mac Conaill's ability to claim the kingship of south Brega. Tigernach defeated Máel-Sechnaill mac Maíle-ruanaid, king of Ireland and Ruarc, king of Bréifne in 846. He defeated the Vikings at Dísert Do-Chonna in 848. St Do-Chonna (alias Mo-Chonna) may have been a patron of the Lagore dynasty since the personal name Gilla Mo-Chonna appears in that dynasty in the eleventh century.[11] That the Vikings had desecrated Do-Chonna's shrine on Inis Pátraic (probably St Patrick's Island off the coast at Skerries) in 798 may not be unrelated to Tigernach's slaughter of them at Dísert Do-Chonna. However, they were very active in Brega in the 840s. Máel-dúin

11 Gilla Mo-Chonna mac Fogartaig (d. 1013) was king of South Brega. I wish to thank Ailbhe Mac Shamhráin for drawing this name to my attention.

mac Conaill was captured by them in 842. He was not alone in suffering at their hands: Máel-mithig mac Cináeda (844) and Máel-Bresail mac Cernaig, king of Mugdornae (849) were killed by them. Despite his disagreement with Máel-Sechnaill some years earlier, Tigernach joined forces with him to attack the Vikings of Dublin in 849. In face of such a strong king of south Brega, it is likely that Máel-dúin mac Conaill tried to assert his – somewhat weak – claim by creating a kingship focussed on his own royal residence and by coining the title *rí/rex Calatruim* as a consolation prize for loss of the title *rí/rex Locha Gabor*. He was unsucessful as the title never appears again.

THE KINGSHIP OF DÉSSI BREG

The annals[12] chronicle the fortunes of four sons of Báeth mac Dícholla kings of Déssi Breg through the eighth century.[13] Daithgus[14] (d. 732), Uarchride (d. 770) and Echtgus (d. 777) were killed, while Niallgus's obit is included among many other notables in 758. As noted above, Echtgus mac Buith was slain at Calatruim, probably while proclaiming Niall mac Conaill Grant, one of the 'Calatruim dynasty', as king of southern Brega. The genealogies preserved in the Book of Leinster[15] and the Book of Lecan[16] include the pedigrees of dynasties descended from Dícuill, apparently known as Uí Dícholla or Uí Rossa, the descendants of Máel-tuili mac Dícholla and Niallgus mac Buith meic Dícholla to the late ninth century, of Ainfíth mac Buith to the early tenth century, of Máel-rubai mac Dícholla to the mid-eleventh century.

It is significant that the genealogies of the native dynasties of Déssi Breg terminate in the eleventh century and this may offer an explanation for the re-appearance in the annals after 250 years of the title *rí Déssi Breg*, when the violent death of Gilla-Fhulartaig king of Déssi Breg in 1034 is noted. His son Muirchertach, *rídomna Déssi Breg*, was killed in 1060. It is likely that the dynasties listed in the Book of Leinster and

12 *AU, Ann. Tig., AFM.*   **13** Note Paul Walsh's comments, 'Meath in Book of Rights', 516.
14 It is worth noting the existence of the frequent occurrence of personal names ending in
-*gus* among the descendants of Dícuill: Daithgus, Niallgus, Echtgus, Dondgus, Lulgus,
Fiangus, Diangus. **15** *Book of Leinster*, ed. Anne O'Sullivan, vi (Dublin, 1983), 1465
(335c35–61).   **16** Book of Lecan 101vd-102ra-b.

Table 2.3 Déssi Breg – the descendants of Báeth son of Dícuill

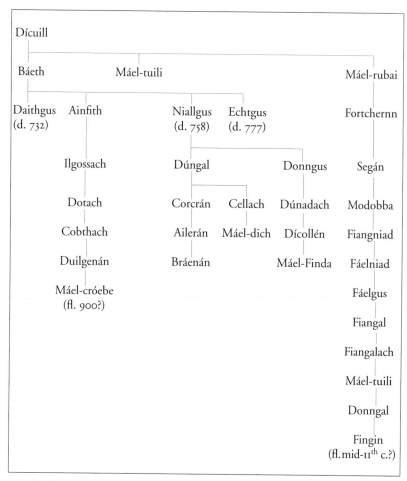

Book of Lecan genealogies continued to hold the title during the period of silence (777–1034) and that, contrary to my opinion expressed in an earlier paper,[17] there is reason to believe that the kingship was usurped by intruders in 1034. The personal names Gilla-Fhulartaig and Fulartach are uncommon and do not appear in the Déssi Breg genealogies. Fulartach is the name of a poet to whom a number of *dindshenchas* poems are attributed.[18] The pedigree of a saint Fulartach of Dál nAraide

17 Bhreathnach, 'Tara and its hinterland', 1. 18 E.J. Gwynn, *The Metrical Dindshenchus*, 5 vols (Dublin, 1903–35).

whose church was Dísert Fhulartaig in Uí Failge is included in the corpus of saints' pedigrees.[19] The occurrence of kings in eleventh century Brega whose families could have come originally from Leinster and who intruded into – or were imposed on – Brega is a phenomenon of the early decades of the eleventh-century. Donnchad úa Duinn *rí Breg* was killed by Róen *rí Mide* in 1027. In 1029 Amlaíb mac Sitriuc, king of Dublin was captured by Mathgamain úa Riacáin, *rí Breg*, to whom a large ransom was paid for his release. Domnall úa Cellaig, undoubtedly the rightful claimant to the kingship of Brega since he belonged to the 'Knowth dynasty', killed Mathgamain úa Riacáin in 1032. It may be no coincidence that Gilla-Sechnaill mac Gilla Mo-Chonna, king of south Brega, was killed in the same year as Gilla-Fhulartaig (1034). It is possible that the latter had come with other families from Uí Failge as planters in Brega and had attempted to usurp the over-kingships of Brega and the kingships of south Brega and Déssi Breg. While the Uí Duinn and Uí Riacáin were unsuccessful in their attempts, the descendants of Gilla-Fhulartaig were more successful since *AFM* record in 1130 that Tigernán Ua Ruairc won a battle at Slíab Guaire (in the Barony, Clankee, Co. Cavan) over the men of Meath. Among those killed at the battle, presumably as part of the army of the king of Mide, Diarmait Ua Máel-Sechnaill, was the son of Gilla-Fhulartaig, king of south Brega.

THE KINGSHIP OF MUGDORNAE BREG

The Mugdornae, one of the components of the confederation known as the Airgialla, were divided into two kingdoms, Mugdornae Maigen whose caput was in the vicinity of Domnach Maigen (Donaghmoyne, Co. Monaghan) and Mugdornae Breg who were connected with the churches of Slane, Co. Meath, Domnach Mór Maige Laithbe (Donaghmore, Co. Meath) and Cell Foibrich (Kilbrew, Co. Meath).[20] An over-kingship of the Mugdornae also existed, on occasion indicated

---

19 Pádraig Ó Riain (ed.), *Corpus genealogiarum sanctorum Hiberniae* (Dublin, 1985), 17 (§103), 193 n.103, index 321. **20** M.A. O'Brien (ed.), *Corpus genealogiarum Hiberniae* (Dublin, 1962; reprint 1976), 152: 142b31–42); F.J. Byrne and P. Francis, 'Two lives of Saint Patrick: Vita Secunda and Vita Quarta', *RSAI Jnl.*, 124 (1994), 5–117: 100.

in the annals by the title *rí/ rex Mugdornae n-uile*.[21] Their lands may have been dispersed through an area extending from south Brega north-westwards to Domnach Maigen. The site of the crannóg of Moynagh Lough close to Nobber, Co. Meath, if identified as Loch Dé Muinech,[22] was *i tírib Mugdorne* 'in the lands of the Mugdornae'.[23] The pedigrees of the dominant dynasty of Mugdornae Maigen, who seem to have consistently held the over-kingship, from Eochu Doimléin (prehistoric) to Máel-ruanaid mac Gilla-Chiaráin (d. 1110) are those preserved in the pre-Norman in the Book of Leinster[24] and the Book of Lecan.

The kings of Mugdornae Breg appear sporadically in the annals and are distinguished by personal names from the Mugdornae Maigen whose kings took names such as Al, Máel-áil, Aléne. The Mugdornae Maigen adopted the surname Ua Machainén, descendants of their king Machainén mac Suibne (*floruit* in the late ninth century).[25] As no continuous genealogy of the dynasties of Mugdornae Breg exist, it is not clear if their kings who are noticed in the annals were related. The earliest reference to a king of Mugdornae Breg is to Rechtabrat mac Dúnchon who was killed in 759. Catharne, slain along with Rímid mac Cernaig (perhaps of Síl nÁedo Sláine – possible son of Cernach of Fir Chúl (d. 766)) at the battle of Cenond fought between the two north-eastern dynasties of Uí Echach Cobo and Conaille Muirthemne in 786, may have been the king of Mugdornae Breg since his name does not appear in the extensive Mugdornae Maigen genealogies. Whether he was or not, the alliance between the Mugdornae and Síl nÁedo Sláine was a feature of eastern and midland politics even after the rest of the Airgialla allied themselves to Cenél nEogain in the ninth century.[26] Cernach mac Flaithnia, king of Mugdornae Breg, died in 812.[27] As noted previously the Vikings were particularly active in Brega in the mid-ninth century and the Mugdornae were not spared. In 837, when the Vikings brought fleet up the Boyne and the Liffey and plundered Mag Life and Mag mBreg, they were defeated by the men of Brega at Deoninne in the lands

---

21 *AU* 834. **22** Edel Bhreathnach, 'Topographical note: Moynagh Lough, Nobber, Co. Meath', *Ríocht na Midhe,* 9, no. 4 (1998), 16–19. **23** O'Brien, *Corpus Geneal. Hib.,* 396 (LL 327h 45). **24** Ibid., 437 (LL 338e 24); Lecan 79 Vdb 33. **25** Machainén is not mentioned in the annals, but the obit of his brother Óengus is recorded in 850. **26** Byrne and Francis, 'Two lives of Patrick', 100. **27** *AU, AFM.*

Table 2.4 *Mugdornae Maigen*

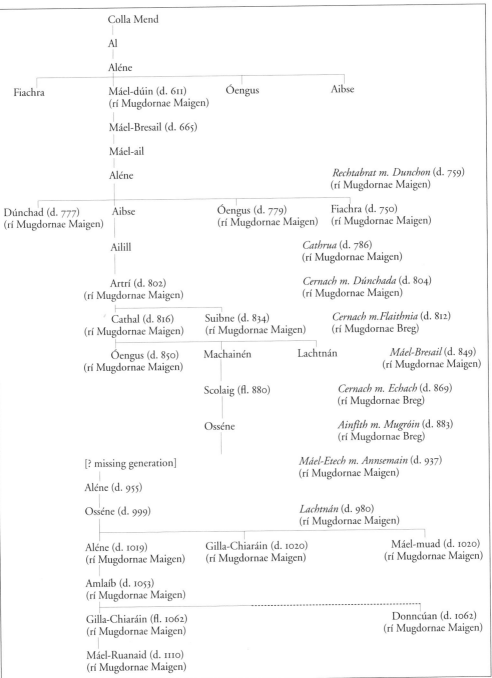

of Mugdornae Breg. Cernach mac Echach (d. 869) and Anfith mac Mugróin (d. 883) are the last kings of Mugdornae Breg to be mentioned in the annals and while they may have continued to rule their lands in Brega, they seem to have been eclipsed by the Uí Machainén kings of Mugdornae Maigen. The latter would appear to have been in alliance with the Uí Chathasaig, kings of the south Brega dynasty of Saithne. In 1019 Aléne mac Osséne úa Machainéin and Osséne Ua Cathasaig were killed by the Gailenga.[28] Aléne's brothers fared no better: in 1020 Gilla-Chiaráin was killed by Fir Rois and Máel-muad by Uí Maic Uais Breg.

THE KINGSHIP OF UÍ MAIC UAIS BREG

In his note on the Uí Maic Uais, Paul Walsh says little of Uí Maic Uais Breg and concentrates on the northern Uí Maic Uais dynasties of Uí Tuirtri, Uí Fiachach Arda Sratha and Uí Meic Cáirthinn.[29] He quotes the Middle Irish poem *Airgialla a hEamain Macha* which fits the Uí Maic Uais Breg into the overall genealogical schema by making them descendants of Forgo son of Cáirthenn (from whom are descended the Uí Meic Cáirthinn). However, as noted by Walsh, no pedigree of the Uí Maic Uais Breg or Uí Meic Uais Mide survives. The pedigree that survives is that of Crichán mac Cathasaig who was king of Uí Maic Uais (d. 719) and who belonged to Uí Fiachrach Arda Sratha. The annals designate three kingships of Uí Maic Uais: Uí Maic Uais ind Fhochla, which must have comprised of the northern branches listed above, Uí Maic Uais Mide whose kingdom lay around the barony of Moygish, Co. Westmeath[30] and Uí Maic Uais Breg. Paul Walsh suggested that the kingdoms of Gailenga Becca and Uí Maic Uais Breg overlapped since a dynasty known as Uí Óengusa is linked to both people in the sources

---

28 *AU*. It may be no coincidence that the Saithne king bore a personal name traditionally associated with Mugdornae Maigen. Although there is no direct evidence, it is possible that his mother was of the Mugdornae and as is so many similar cases introduced a name from her own family into her adopted family. **29** Paul Walsh, 'Uí Maccu Uais', *Ériu*, 9 (1921–3), 55–60. Reprinted in Nollaig Ó Muraíle (ed.), *Irish leaders and learning through the ages* (Dublin, 2003), 68–72. I use the later form of the name Uí Maic Uais throughout. **30** Their kings were Uí Minnegáin (*AFM* 1106) and Uí Cormaide (*AFM* 1152).

and Cell Sinche (Kilshine, barony of Morgallion, Co. Meath) is said to have been in the territory of Uí Maic Uais Breg.[31] The version of *Lebor Gabála Érenn* in the Book of Leinster claims that Loch Laíglinne was *la Hú Mac Cuais Breg*,[32] although the *dindshenchas* poem on Loch Laíglinne does not specify the lake's location.[33] It may be that, in a manner similar to Mugdornae, Uí Maic Uais Breg did not rule a kingdom concentrated on one location, but held lands throughout Brega and Mide. While no pedigree of Uí Maic Uais Breg survives, the fortunes of their ruling dynasty can be re-constructed from the annals for the late eighth to the early tenth century (see table 2.5):

Table 2.5 Kings of Uí Maic Uais Breg, c.720–c.937

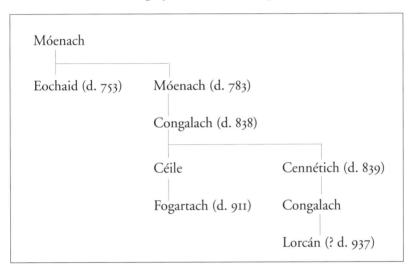

It seems that internecine strife struck this family in the mid-ninth century: Congalach mac Móenaig died suddenly in 838 and his son Cennétech who succeeded him was killed by another son Céile in 839. Céile's son Fogartach died as king in 911 and he seems to have been succeeded by his cousin once-removed Lorcán mac Congalaig (d. 935).

31 Walsh, 'Meath in the Book of Rights', 520; Ó Muraíle (ed.), *Irish leaders*, 84.   **32** R. I. Best, Osbern Bergin and M.A. O'Brien (eds), *The Book of Leinster formerly Lebar na Núachongbála*, i (Dublin, 1954), 16: 5a 481.   **33** Edward Gwynn (ed.), *The Metrical Dindshenchas* Part iv (Dublin, 1924; reprinted 1991), 256.

Two further kings of Uí Maic Uais Breg are noted, Muiredach Ua Duibeoin (d. 1017) and Cellach mac Muirecáin (d. 1058). It is unclear if they were the descendants of earlier kings or even if they were related. The existence of the personal name Muirecán among the northern Uí Thuirtri raises the suspicion that either Cellach's designation as king of Uí Maic Uais Breg is incorrect or that the northern branch of Uí Maic Uais usurped the title in the twelfth century. This may have occurred in the wake of the raid made by Lethlobar mac Laidgnéin (of Fernmaige),[34] king of the Airgialla against the men of Mide and Brega, and particularly against the Gailenga in 1053.[35] This possible usurpation may also have been an attempt to counter the claims of the Uí Óengusa, who may have been Gailenga Becca, to the kingship of Uí Maic Uais.[36]

The relationship between the various Uí Maic Uais Breg branches and other eastern, midlands and northern dynasties is sketchy. The dynamic of the Uí Maic Uais over-kingship is not as clear as that of the Mugdornae. It would appear that kings accorded the various titles *rex nepotum moccu (maic) Uais, rex nepotum filiorum (C)uais (AU), tighearna Uí Mic Uais (AFM)* held the over-kingship of the northern branches, but may not have always been able to rule the southern branches of Uí Maic Uais Breg and Mide. A small number of eleventh-century entries in the annals offer some impression of relations with other dynasties. In 1017 Muiredach Ua Duibeoin, king of Uí Maic Uais Breg, was killed by Flaithbertach Ua Néill of Cenél nÉogain who had come to Mide to assist Máel-Sechnaill mac Domnaill (d. 1022). Muiredach's death may have been part of a campaign waged by Cenél nÉogain to subdue difficult elements in Brega. For example, in 1018, they came to Cell Foibrich (Kilbrew, Co. Meath) – a church with Mugdornae connections – and killed a large number of people there. It is clear from concentrating on the smaller kingships of Brega that at a more local level relations among them could occasionally be fraught. The events of 1019–20 in which three kings of Mugdornae Maigen were killed have been cited in the previous section

34 cf. O'Brien, *Corpus Geneal. Hib.*, 184 (Rawlinson B 502, 146e 30).   35 *AFM*; Ann. Tig.
36 Walsh, 'Meath in the Book of Rights', 520. Walsh notes the obit of Madadán Ua Óengusa, lord of Gailenga Becca and Fir Chúl in 1003 (AFM). He also notes from late medieval topographical poems of Seaán Ó Dubhagáin that Ua hAonghusa were lords of Uí Maic Uais Breg and Gailenga Becca. Of course, by the twelfth century, the kingship of Gailenga or Machaire Gailenga had been usurped by the Uí Ragellaig.

as an indication of the tangled web of alliances that existed at local level. That the Gailenga killed Aléne mac Osséne in 1019 and the Uí Maic Uais Breg Máel-muad mac Osséne in 1020 probably reflects the close connection between these people, observed in other sources. The third party in the alliance against Mugdornae Maigen at the time were Fir Rois who killed Gilla-Chiaráin mac Osséne in 1020. The killing of the king of Saithne during the same series of events suggests that the emergence of the Saithne was probably resented by people such as the Gailenga and Uí Maic Uais whose kingdoms were being encroached upon by the increasingly powerful dynasty of Uí Cathasaig kings of Saithne. Evidence of this expansionist policy can be detected by the title accorded to Máel-Chiarán Ua Cathasaig on his death at the battle of Crincha at Dublin in 1086. He is styled king of Brega (*AU*) and king of Saithne and Túath Luigne (*AFM*).

CONCLUSION

These brief notes are a contribution towards understanding the detailed operation of kingship in early medieval Ireland. Royal titles, often short-lived, could be created as part of internecine conflict over a more important kingship such as the over-kingship of Brega or the kingship of south Brega. Old kingships or sub-kingships could be usurped and taken from their rightful owners, a phenomenon particularly prevalent in the eleventh century. Finally, provincial and regional kings such as the kings of Brega or emerging kingdoms such as Saithne needed the support of lesser kings who continued to have the power to promote their masters or to cause their downfall. This sketch of some lesser kingships in Brega offers an insight into the dynamics of the polity of that region from the late seventh century to the twelfth century.

ACKNOWLEDGMENTS

I wish to thank Dr Paul Byrne for his detailed comments on this paper, and the editor for his comments and assistance with the genealogical charts.

An ecclesiastical enclosure in the townland of Grange, parish of Holmpatrick

AILBHE MAC SHAMHRÁIN

Evidence for ecclesiastical settlement, of presumed medieval or Early Christian date, has long been recognised in the townland of Grange, adjacent to Milverton Desmesne. The 'Record of Monuments and Places' (RMP) at Dúchas documents an ecclesiastical complex within the townland, consisting of an old burial ground, within which stands the remains of a church building, while there is holy well nearby.[1] The curving shape of townland boundaries between Grange and Balcunnin to the south and Killalane to the west, and the presence of a stream to the north, are suggestive of an ecclesiastical enclosure. However, as all surface traces had long been removed, no precise data was available in relation to the enclosure until its form was brought to light by geo-physical survey in the spring of 2003.

Of the church itself, only the foundations survive. The building was small and rectangular in plan, measuring approximately 10m x 8m, with an entrance in western end of the southern wall. A simple structure, consisting of a nave without a chancel, it was built mainly of roughly-coursed stonework with a rubble core although large boulders were used in the northern wall.[2] Small simple church buildings are often assumed to be early, but such scant remains do little to facilitate dating on the basis of architectural style. A few years ago, during a clean-up at the site, a sherd of pottery of thirteenth-century date was found in the rubble core – but whether this attests to building or repair work at that time, or was deposited there at a later date, is uncertain.

The holy well, concerning which folk-custom and belief survived into the twentieth century, is located near the stream to the north of the site.

---

1 RMP DU 005: 024/01–04; NGR (National Grid reference) 32256/25919; see Geraldine Stout & Matthew Stout, 'Patterns in the past: Co. Dublin 5000 BC to 1000 AD', in F.H.A. Aalen & K. Whelan (eds), *Dublin city and county from prehistory to the present: studies in honour of J.H. Andrews* (Dublin, 1992), appendix v, 33. 2 RMP DU 005: 024/01.

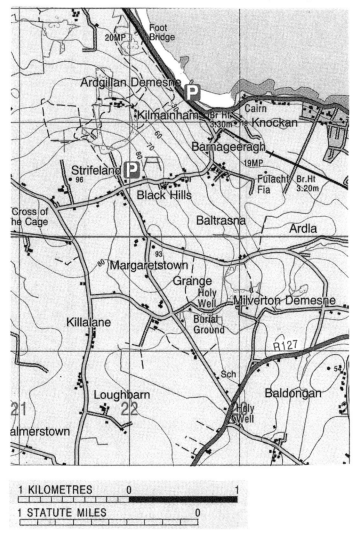

3.1 Ecclesiastical site at Grange and the surrounding townlands based on
Ordnance Survey Ireland Permit no. 7713.
© Ordnance Survey Ireland and Government of Ireland

Reached by a footpath, the entrance to which is opposite the Milverton
Hall gate lodge, this well – or spring – lies within a circular enclosure a
little over 1m in diameter. It is surmounted by a horseshoe-shaped cairn
of large boulders – 6m long, 2.4m wide and 1.50m high. Set into the
north wall of the well structure, is a 'bullaun stone'. Like most of its
class, it is roughly circular in shape with a concave bowl carved out of its

flattened upper surface. Bullauns, a common feature of Early Christian sites, remain enigmatic; they may have been used as baptismal fonts. Suggestions to the effect that the 'holy well' tradition had its origin with recourse to sacred springs in the pre-Christian era appear attractive, but for want of further investigation remain unprovable. This particular well was formerly resorted to for cure of a range of minor ailments, including warts, toothache, headache and sore throat; there was also a tradition concerning an irreverent ploughman who, on being warned not to till the field adjacent to the well because it was the holy ground of St Movee, boldly responded, 'St Movee or St Movoe, I'll cut this frough before I go' – at which point the ground opened and swallowed man, horse and plough![3]

The traditional association of the well and burial ground with St Movee, presumably an Early Christian cult-figure included among the 'saints of the Irish tradition', suggests a pre-Norman date for the site. However, some difficulties have been encountered in seeking to identify the indivdual concerned. Given the relative proximity of Grange to Glasnevin, there is an understandable tendency to identify its patron with Mo-bí of Glas Naíden,[4] whose existence is well attested in the historical record. Known as Mo-bí *Cláraínech* (the table-faced), or as Berchán *Cecus* (the blind, or visually-impaired) – Mo-bí is a hypochoristic, or 'familiar' form of Berchán – he is traced to the Connacht population group of Corco Thrí, located in the barony of Corann, Co. Sligo.[5] In a seemingly anachronistic episode, he is brought into contact with Cóemgen (St Kevin) of Glendalough, whose death might reasonably be placed around 620, although according to the annals Mo-bí died of 'in bléfed' (the plague) in 545 – presumably on 12 October, under which date he is commemorated in the martyologies.[6]

However, the eminent nineteenth-century antiquarian, Bishop William Reeves, in discussing the identity of St Dúilech – founder of Clochar

---

3 Caoimhín Ó Danachair, 'The holy wells of Co. Dublin', *Reportorium Novum*, 2, no. 1 (1958), 73; NGR 32256/25938. **4** This is suggested in the RMP; DU 005: 024/02. **5** LL 351g 20; *Book of Leinster*, ed. Anne O'Sullivan, vi (Dublin, 1983), 1567; Pádraig Ó Riain (ed.), *Corpus Genealogiarum Sanctorum Hiberniae* (Dublin, 1985), 44. **6** Vita Sancti Coemgeni, §30; Charles Plummer (ed.), *Vitae Sanctorum Hiberniae*, i (Oxford, 1910), 249–50; the episode, in which Cóemgen visits Berchán/Mo-bí on his return journey from having met St Garbán at Kinsaley, implies that Glasnevin is the intended venue – not Grange/Milverton; see *AU* 545; *AU* 618/622 for Cóemgen; see Martyrology of Tallaght, *Bk. Leinster*, vi, 1639; *Félire Óengusso Céli Dé*, ed. Whitley Stokes (London, 1905) at 12 October.

Dúilig (St Doolagh's, Malahide Road) – is adamant that 'Movee' of Grange is not the saint of Glasnevin, but Mo-báe moccu Aldai.[7] Of course, Mo-báe (with a variant form Mo-bóe) and Mo-bí are separate names – but are sufficiently similar to prompt confusion. One recalls the above-mentioned folk tale, in which the ploughman expressed his contempt for the 'holy ground' of 'St Movee or St Movoe' – which may hint at some fusion of cults at popular level. Mo-báe is the hypochoristic form of Báetán, and the Báetán in question here was, according to the genealogies of the Irish saints, a son of Sinell son of Nad-fraích, making him a kinsman of Dúilech – an uncle, if the genealogies may be taken at face-value.[8] These two local cult-figures belonged to the Conmaicne; the best-known branch of this population group, known as Conmaicne Mara, leaves its name on the district of Connemara, Co. Galway, but various other branches were scattered across Ireland from west to east with some located in Co. Meath.[9] Báetán moccu Aldai died in 630, his feast-day being noted in the martyrologies at 13 December.[10] He is associated with a foundation called Cluain dá Andobair (or Cluain Fannabair, which represents a variant of the former) in the territory of Uí Muiredaig, identified as Cloney, Co. Kildare.[11] The surviving sources provide no evidence that this Báetán was connected with any other site; the list of homonymous saints features eleven by the name of Mo-báe (or Mo-bóe – most of whom are identifiable), including two associated with *Coill* and with *Leth* – seemingly placenames, but completely obscure.[12] The link between Mo-báe and Grange, therefore, is not attested in hagiography – that genre of literature concerned with the saints and their (alleged) doings. This being the case, Reeves does not explain how the local patron-saint can be identified as Mo-báe; perhaps traditions concerning 'Movoe' were still remembered locally in the mid-nineteenth century, or the 'pattern' was still held at the holy well on the latter's feast-day, 13 December.

7 William Reeves, 'A memoir of the church of St Dúilech', *RIA Proc.*, 7 (1861), 141–7: 142. **8** Ó Riain (ed.), *Corpus Geneal. SS Hib.*, 22. **9** Ibid., 194, notes 128, 129; Edmund Hogan, *Onomasticon Goedelicum* (London 1910; reprinted Dublin, 2000), 289; Francis John Byrne, *Irish kings and high kings*, new ed. (Dublin, 2001), 68. **10** *Ann. Tig.* at 630; *Fél. Óeng.; Félire Huí Gormáin*, ed. Whitley Stokes (London, 1895); *The Martyrology of Donegal*, ed. J. O'Donovan, J.H. Todd & W. Reeves (Dublin, 1864) at 13 December. **11** See O'Donovan et al., *Mart. Donegal*; Hogan, *Onomasticon Goedelicum*; Liam Price, index to Charles McNeill (ed.), *Calendar of Archbishop Alen's Register* (Dublin, 1950), 327. **12** LL 368e 1–11; O'Sullivan (ed.), *Bk. Leinster*, vi, 1670; Ó Riain (ed.), *Corpus Geneal. SS Hib.*, 151, 319, 327 (index).

Over the years, various indications have been noted that ecclesiastical settlement probably extended beyond the surviving complex of field monuments. Folk tradition in the area long maintained that a field adjoining the burial ground, known as the 'Church Field', had been used for the interment of plague or famine victims at some indeterminate period in the past A sincere respect for such unmarked burials doubtless underlay the story of the recalcitrant ploughman. There is another holy well, known as 'Lady Well' in the adjacent townland of Balcunnin where, up to the twentieth century, a 'pattern day' was held on 1 May.[13] Although this date later acquired an association with the Virgin Mary, in Early Christian Ireland it marked the feast-day of at least eleven native 'saints'. Of more specific archaeological interest was the discovery, in 1991, of a slab-lined grave in low-lying field just north of the burial ground of St Movee, but situated within the adjacent townland of Margaretstown.[14] Having come to light in the course of building work, the grave took the form of a pit dug into boulder clay, measuring 1.7m in length with a maximum width of 0.4m, narrowing to 0.3m towards its eastern end. It was aligned on an east-west axis, and was lined with limestone slabs. There were no finds accompanying the burial – the only artifacts discovered being three pieces of unworked flint pebbles and a retouched piece, which were found in a disturbed context. This absence of grave-goods, in conjunction with an east-west alignment, suggests an Early Christian date, possibly between the ninth and eleventh centuries AD. Another possible burial, this time east of the Grange complex in the townland of Milverton, may be indicated by a stray find reported in 1986. This comprised a skull fragment, portion of a human cranium, found in ploughsoil within a field known as the 'Danes Burial Ground'.[15] These burials, occurring at some distance from the surviving church ruin and burial ground, suggest the possibility that ecclesiastical settlement, in the medieval period, spread over a wider area.

---

13 RMP DU 005: 036; Ó Danachair, 'Holy wells of Co. Dublin', 73. **14** RMP DU 005: 055; Geraldine Stout, 'Margaretstown: slab-lined grave', in Isabel Bennett (ed.), *Excavations 1991* (Dublin, 1992), 17–18. Osteoarchaeologist Laureen Buckley, in an unpublished skeletal report, commented on the bone remains which consisted of four pieces of long bone – shaft portions of the right and left femur and tibia. On the basis of diameter measurements and the lack of strong muscle insertions, she concluded that the individual was a young female – perhaps only sixteen to twenty years of age. **15** National Museum Topographical Files, 1986: 140.

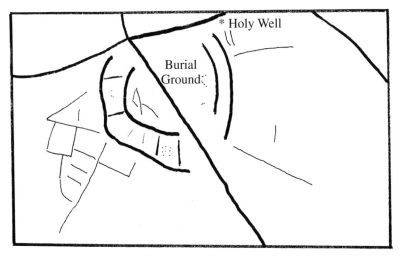

3.2 Outline of the enclosure at Grange

In view of such indications of wider settlement, detection through geophysical survey, carried out by archaeological consultants in May 2003, of a large double enclosure surrounding the ecclesiastical complex is of major importance. While the report has yet to be made available, a published photograph (upon which the accompanying figure is based), illustrates some of the more pertinent geophysical images.[16] The survey reveals an inner enclosure with an estimated diameter of 100m, within which the church ruin and present burial ground is situated, and an outer enclosure of up to 200m across. This extended site is bisected by a road, which links the R 127 with the old road from Skerries via Strifeland to Balrothery. On the eastern side, part of the site is covered by the burial ground and by development immediately north of its perimeter and so does not feature in the survey. An interesting feature is the presence of several radial lines (four on the west side are especially clear) between the inner and outer enclosures. These are enigmatic, but appear to demarcate sections within the complex. Sectional divisions of this order (if that is what they are) are not a familiar feature of Irish ecclesiastical sites; pending further investigation of this phenomenon, there may be a case for re-examination of some known sites using geophysical techniques.[17] Also

16 *Archaeology Ireland*, 17, no. 2 (Summer 2003), 40.   **17** The occurrence of radial lines between the inner and outer enclosure is of particular interest in the light of recent discoveries

revealed by the survey was an annexed network of rectilinear enclosures, but whether these are indicative of agricultural or industrial activity is not apparent. There is a need for further investigation of archaeological features within the enclosure and for the publication of a report, which would include analysis of possible structures and of activity on the site – to include ritual, agricultural and industrial.

However, on the basis of what is presently known, it is clear that Grange was the focus of a major ecclesiastical settlement. Yet, in common with a great many ecclesiastical sites, it seems to have found no place in pre-Norman historical sources. Neither Grange nor any of the adjacent locations, including the townlands of Milverton and Killalane (along with Balcunnin, Baltrasna and Margaretstown) feature in the annals – at least not under the names by which they are now known. The townland name of Killalane prompts comparison with Killelane (a site adjacent to the priory of St Saviour, Glendalough), the Irish form of which was Cell Fáeláin, dedicated to Fáelán, son of the holy widow Caintigern, whose cult was well established in Scotland and occurs in eastern Ireland – at Glendalough and at Cluain Mo-escna in Fartullagh, Co. Westmeath.[18] Still, if there was a foundation known as Cell Fáeláin in the vicinity – whether or not it can be identified with the site at Grange – it is completely undocumented. In the later medieval period, the lands of Grange were included in the estate of the Augustinian priory of St Patrick, founded *c*.1220. Following the dissolution of the monasteries, a jury reported that the priory church of Holmpatrick was 'parochial from time immemorial'; Grange (Newegraunge) and several surrounding townlands, including Milverton (Milwardiston), formed part of this parish but, apparently, by that time, its ecclesiastical settlement had faded from the landscape. [19]

The apparent absence of the ecclesiastical complex at Grange from the historical record certainly does not mean that the site was insignificant.

at Oldtown, near Swords, where remote sensing of lands also identified such lines. The same site has also produced burials (Geraldine Stout, personal communication, 18 September 2003). **18** Liam Price, *The placenames of Co. Wicklow* (Dublin, 1942), i, 36: Ailbhe MacShamhráin, *Church and polity in pre-Norman Ireland: the case of Glendalough* (Maynooth, 1996), 132. Alternatively, the Fáelán intended may be the individual commemorated at 31 October *Féil. Óeng.*, where a gloss identifies him as a brother of St Fursu and abbot (of Fosse) in Gaul. **19** *Extents of Irish monastic possessions, 1540–1541*, ed. Newport White (Dublin, 1943), 49, 50; A. Gwynn & R.N. Hadcock, *Medieval religious houses: Ireland*, new ed. (Dublin, 1988), 154, 178.

While discussion of possible structures at the site, or indeed dwelling areas, must await the production of a report, the dimensions of the enclosure alone make it clear that this was a centre of considerable importance and probably supported a sizeable population of clerics and ecclesiastical tenants. It is hardly the case that Grange failed to develop in socio-economic terms. At the time of writing, data attesting to other industrial activity at Grange is not available, but it has been known since the mid-nineteenth century that milling was carried out at, or near, the site. In 1848, while supervising drainage works near St Movee's Well, George Woods discovered, in a watercourse, several dams of yellow clay, a millshaft and several grindstones.[20] These he presented to the Royal Irish Academy. In 1851 two millstones came to light in Milverton Demesne, which were donated to the Museum (along with some skulls) but were not recorded in the topographical files. The recorded description of these finds accords well with accounts of horizontal mills excavated in recent decades and dated by radio-carbon testing to the eighth and ninth centuries AD. Mills of this kind, their horizontal wheels driven by water channeled from a millpond (generally formed by damming a small stream), ground a range of cereals. They are particularly associated with ecclesiastical settlements, and it is clear from the 'lives of the saints' that they provided a 'semi-public' facility, grinding corn for the tenantry of the church's estates.[21]

A settlement the size of Grange, which almost certainly served a range of social and commercial – in addition to purely ecclesiastical – functions, is unlikely to have been ephemeral. On the contrary, it probably developed over a lengthy period of time. Especially as it lacks an historical record, it is almost impossible, without excavation, to assign a foundation date. As the Early Christian cult-figure most likely commemorated here, Mo-báe moccu Aldai, died in 630 it can hardly be earlier than seventh century – but could well be later. Finds of what appear to have been horizontal mills, and the slab-lined grave outside the (modern) burial ground, suggest occupation at (or near) the site at any stage between the

---

20 A.T. Lucas, 'The horizontal mill in Ireland', *RSAI Jnl.*, 83 (1953), 1–36: 5, 35. **21** See e.g. Colin Rynne, 'Archaeology and the early Irish water mill', *Archaeology Ireland*, 3, no. 3 (Autumn 1989), 110–14; Idem, 'Milling in the seventh century', *Archaeology Ireland*, 6, no. 2 (Summer 1992), 22–4.

seventh century and the eleventh. The pottery sherd found in the core of the church wall, mentioned above, seems to indicate activity of some kind as late as the thirteenth century – but the fact that it was neither a parish church nor a priory in the post-Norman period probably means that it had lost importance as a religious centre, population-focus or commercial venue. In view of the Anglo-Norman tendency to adopt existing centres, it seems likely that Grange had declined by the twelfth century – when the territorialization of dioceses was driving the formation of deaneries and parishes.

In the final analysis, the failure of a large and (apparently) economically-developed centre like Grange to feature in pre-Norman historical sources is difficult to explain satisfactorily. It is a question of the survival of chronicles, and of the likely recording centres for the strata of annals discernible in the compilations left to us. If there ever was a local record for Fingal, it is lost. Most of the annal-entries relating to the area are a legacy, it seems, from an Uí Néill recording centre in the east midlands. It is salutary to note that in the area between the Broad Meadow Water and the Delvin – the local kingdom of Saithne – only two ecclesiastical sites have any annal-record; these are Lusk and Inis Pátraic, both of which had close connections with Síl nÁeda Sláine, an Uí Néill dynasty.[22] Perhaps the foundation at Grange was independent of the Uí Néill overlords – its senior clergy drawn from local Saithne aristocracy – in which event the Meath-based chroniclers, whose record survives, were disinclined to document its affairs.

ACKNOWLEDGMENTS

The writer is grateful to Dr Conchubhar Ó Crualaoich of the Placenames Offices, and to Dr Geraldine Stout of Dúchas, for various helpful comments and suggestions – but is alone responsible for any views and opinions expressed here.

This paper, first written in Autumn 2003, is included here in place of the contribution that would have been made by Leo Swan, had he lived.

22 See below, MacShamhráin, 'Church and dynasty in Early Christian Brega'; in addition, two other sites in the area, Rush and Bremore, find mention in the martyrologies.

St Patrick, Skerries and the earliest evidence for local church organization in Ireland

CATHERINE SWIFT

The oldest account of Patrick's visit to Skerries comes from a late seventh-century writer, Bishop Tírechán, who wrote an account of Patrick's travels in Ireland some time around the 670s AD. According to Tírechán, Inispatrick 'the island of Patrick' was the first site that Patrick visited on his return to Ireland as a missionary after he had escaped from his slavery. His exact words (in translation of the original Latin) run as follows:

> In fact, Patrick came with Gauls to the islands of the Moccu Chor and [he was] at the eastern island which is called the Island of Patrick and with him was a crowd of holy bishops and priests and deacons and exorcists, door-keepers, readers and young boys whom he had ordained. For he came from the sea to the plain of Brega [otherwise Mag mBreg] at sun-rise with the blessing of God, with the true light of miraculous doctrine, lighting the thick clouds of ignorance.[1]

Bishop Tírechán's text survives in a single manuscript; a small copy of the Four Gospels written for the leader of Patrick's community at Armagh some time around the beginning of the ninth century. It forms part of a collection of texts about Patrick and his cult which is inserted at the beginning of the manuscript which today is known as the Book of Armagh. A fundamental question for students of Patrick is to try and determine the status of these documents; when and where they were written and for what purpose.

---

1 The translation is my own from J. Gwynn's diplomatic transcription in *Liber Ardmachanus; the Book of Armagh* (Dublin, 1913), f.9rb 38–9va 5. The translations provided in L. Bieler, *The Patrician texts in the Book of Armagh* (Dublin 1979) do not make sufficient allowance for the influence of Old Irish on Tírechán's Latin.

The context for such enquiries was outlined by Donnchadh Ó Corráin in a paper given in Oxford in which he stated:

> The greater part of the texts we possess are the books of caste; the work books (or rather copies of them) of practicing literate specialists in a quasi-literate society. These are not meant for profane eyes. In very many instances the matter is not in the form in which it was – or could be – delivered to the consumer.[2]

Obviously this description is not of the great illuminated gospel books such as the Book of Kells but deals instead with the manuscripts in which our sagas, genealogies and laws are found transcribed. The classification of many of these as jotters – in which written materials could be summarised for oral use – makes a great deal of sense when one considers the amount of investment in time and materials which is required before one can encrypt information on a piece of parchment. The calves or sheep have to be skinned and the skins left in a lime bath for some weeks; then stretched, dried, cut up and sewn together in the form of a book; oak apples, holly leaves, soot and egg-whites have to be collected and treated in order to produce the ink and so forth. In addition, the scribe has to be taught how to read and write and he has to master these skills in at least two languages, Latin and Irish. In short, a large number of people and a great deal of resources have already been involved before the scribe can sit down to his task. Thus, if we consider the economic value of the manuscript in its blank state, it follows that any information written upon it, however muddled, self-contradictory or unfinished it might appear to modern eyes, is likely to have also been considered valuable and must be treated as such by modern scholars.

This is well recognized in modern Irish literary studies. It used to be argued that many of our surviving sagas were simply ham-fisted renditions of half-remembered primeval stories, as told by *seanchaithe* around the fires of prehistoric Ireland. More recently, scholars such as Máire Herbert in Cork or Caoimhín Breatnach in Dublin, have emphasized the extent

---

2 D. Ó Corráin, 'Historical need and literary narrative', in D. Ellis Evans, J.G. Griffith & E.M. Jope (eds), *Proceedings of the Seventh International Congress of Celtic Studies Oxford 1983* (Oxford, 1986), 141–58, 142.

to which each saga or version of a saga has to be considered in its own right as a product of tenth-, twelfth- or sixteenth-century Ireland. Among those who study St Patrick, however, much of the modern discourse is still being framed in the late nineteenth-century context provided by Eoin Mac Neill and John Gwynn. MacNeill and those who followed him believed that the Book of Armagh was a collection of fragments rescued from oblivion by wandering Armagh monks; men who wore out large quantities of shoe leather criss-crossing the country, interviewing ancient men at country cross-roads and collecting small bits of mice-eaten parchment in remote churches.[3]

This interpretation of the Book of Armagh material as a whole is based on the evidence of Bishop Tírechán's text in particular. The work, today known as the *Collectanea*, is prefaced by a statement which reads: 'Bishop Tírechán has written this from the mouth or the book of Bishop Ultán whose fosterling and pupil he was.'[4] Within the text itself, there are references to *seniores* or old men who gave him stories about early founders of churches around Kells. He also mentions that he himself had visited various places which he describes, including Tara and various sites in Connacht. From the evidence provided we can deduce that Bishop Tírechán was a native of north Mayo whose church lay to the south-west of Killala Bay while his foster-father was Bishop Ultán Moccu Chonchubair of Ardbraccan, to the west of Navan in Co. Meath. (Ultán's death is recorded in the Annals of Ulster under the year 657.) It seems likely that Tírechán's reliance on Ultán's book is strongest where he talks of Patrick's activity in the areas of Meath and north Dublin.

Some scholars, such as Liam de Paor and Charles Doherty, have argued that Tírechán's entire text is made up of 'wisps' and 'fragments' dating back to the fifth or early sixth century.[5] If this were to be the case, one might expect to see traces of the Irish language of fifth and sixth-century date in the forms of the placenames and personal names which

---

3 See, for example, the articles by Eoin MacNeill summarized in a collection entitled *St Patrick* and edited by J. Ryan (Dublin, 1964). John Gwynn's analysis is to be found in the introduction to his diplomatic edition, *Liber Ardmachanus* (see note 1 above).   **4** *Liber Ardmachanus* f.9rb 1–3.   **5** See L. de Paor, *St Patrick's world* (Dublin, 1993), 38–45, 198; C. Doherty, 'The cult of St Patrick and the politics of Armagh in the seventh century' in J–M Picard (ed.), *Ireland and northern France, AD 600–850* (Dublin, 1991), 53–94.

Tírechán provides. In contrast, however, Fergus Kelly's study of the language of the Patrician texts in the Book of Armagh, published in 1979, suggests that there is no evidence for the incorporation of evidence which long pre-dates Tírechán's own day. Kelly characterized Tírechán's use of Irish in the following terms:

> Tírechán's *Collectanea* contains a greater number of Irish words than Muirchú's *Vita*. The occurrence of archaic ē, ō, ĕ and ŏ indicates that it was composed at approximately the same period.[6]

Elsewhere Kelly classifes Muirchú's Irish as pre AD 700; earlier than the material in the mid-eighth-century Würzburg glosses. This concurs with the fact that we know Muirchú was present at the synod of Birr in 697. The implication of Kelly's comments, therefore, is that there is nothing in Tírechán's use of Early Old Irish forms to suggest a date much earlier than the second half of the seventh century. If his *Collectanea* is made up of 'wisps' and 'fragments' dating back to the fifth or early sixth century, then the type of Irish used indicates that such wisps were substantially rewritten.

Looking at the reference to Inispatrick, there is nothing to suggest that this might be a 'fragment' which long pre-dates the period in which Tírechán and Ultán were working, around the middle of the seventh century. The extract occurs at the very beginning of Tírechán's work and describes Patrick's arrival in Ireland. The list of bishops and other clergy who accompanied him is fundamental to the text as a whole in which Tírechán identifies the various clerics whom Patrick established at churches during his travels through the northern half of Ireland. The image of Patrick arriving on Irish shores at sunrise and dispelling darkness reoccurs at numerous points throughout the work as a metaphor for conversion and it appears to be a theme deriving from Isaiah 9:2: 'The people who walked in darkness have seen a great light; those who dwell in a land of deep darkness, on them has light shined.' In short, the account of Patrick's arrival at Skerries fits neatly into the overall scheme of Tírechán's material.

---

6 F. Kelly, 'Notes on the Irish words' in *The Patrician texts in the Book of Armagh*, ed. L. Bieler (Dublin, 1979), 242–248, 244.

On the other hand, both the composition of the *Collectanea* and the way it is laid out within the Book of Armagh does suggest that, on occasion, Tírechán may be incorporating written material drawn from elsewhere. There are, for example, only two lists of churches, identified by placenames or by personnel, in the whole of his text. One such is the numbered list of churches which begins on the second line of column a, folio 10 recto. A slightly larger DE in the middle of a line within the column, signals the commencement of a new sequence of ideas. It reads as follows:

> About churches which he [that is Patrick] founded in Mag mBreg:
> Firstly in *Cul Mine*
> .ii. church of *Cern-* in which Ercus is buried who *carried* a great
>   plague
> .iii. in the hills of *Ais-*
> .iiii. in *Blaitine*
> .v. in *Collumb* ... in which he ordained Holy Eugenius bishop
> .vi. a church belonging to the son of Lathphe
> .vii. in Brí Dam in which was holy Dulcis, brother of Carthacus
> .viii. above Argetbor in which was bishop Kannanus whom Patrick
>   ordained on the first Easter at the *fertae* [burial mound] of the
>   men of Fíacc ...[7]

The distinctive nature of this list is apparent when we compare it with the only other long list of church sites from Meath, found on folio 11 recto:

> He [Patrick] placed a church above the ford of *Sege* and another church [belonging to?] holy Cinnena above the ford of *Carnoí* in the Boyne and another is above *Coirp Raithe* and another is above the ditch of Dallbronach which the Bishop Mac Cairtin held, the uncle of holy Brigid. And he founded another in *Campus Echredd*, another in *Campus Taidcni* which is called *Cell Bile* (which is held by the community of *Scíre*), another in *Campus Echnach* where Cassanus was priest, another in *Singite*, another in *Campus Bili*

---

7 *Liber Ardmachanus* f.10ra 2–13.

next to the ford of the Dog's Head, another in the Head of Carmellus in *Campus Teloch* in which holy Brigid took the veil from the hands of Mac Caille in *Uisnech* of Mide.[8]

Comparing this list with the first list of churches in Mag mBreg, one notes that the second list does not use numbers to count off the churches. Instead, churches on the second list tend to be identified in each case with a *campus* – a word which Tírechán himself says is a translation of the word *mag* or discrete area of cultivated land.[9] In the first list, two churches are given the simple title *aeclessia*; in both cases, these foundations are connected with named individuals. No church is identified by person alone in the second list which uses placenames and/or a combination of person and place-name. Where place-names are identified in the first list, they are prefixed with the Latin preposition *in* except in those cases where the following word begins with *b* when the Irish preposition *i* is used. (*Argetbor* provides an exceptional case and will be discussed below.) In the second list, the general Latin preposition used is *super* or 'above' apparently a translation of the Irish *for* which can also carry the meaning 'at' or 'upon'.

In five of the eight churches, the Patrician foundations in the first, Mag mBreg list, are identified with localized saints. Two of these saints are bishops, one is the brother of a man identified elsewhere in the *Collectanea* as a bishop and two others are given no title by Tírechán but are identified in other sources as bishops. In contrast, only one settlement is identified in topographical terms – that is the reference to the hills of Ais-. In short, whereas the second list emphasizes the geographical location of the churches, the first list emphasizes the personnel who were associated with them. We have seen that there is nothing in the forms of Irish used to suggest that these lists are much earlier than Tírechán's day but the distinctive nature of the two lists would seem to suggest that he is incorporating information drawn either from Ultán's book or from other sources. Given that the two lists are so different in format, it would seem that even if they both came from Ultán's book, it seems likely that he, in turn, had taken them from two different texts.

8 *Liber Ardmachanus* f.11ra 7–20.　**9** *Liber Ardmachanus* f.12va 22–23.

A key to the understanding of either list is obviously the identification of the place-names involved but this is not as easy as might first appear. As elsewhere, Irish place-name studies has developed in a number of separate directions. On the one hand, the distribution of key elements such as *domnach* or *cell* have been examined for their historical significance – in a manner similar to the debate on *-ham* or *-vik* settlements in England or *papa* in Scotland. On the other there are the geographically-based studies which examine the ancestry of all place-names within a modern administrative unit – as for example, Liam Price's investigations of Wicklow place-names or the current work by the Northern Irish Place-names group under the directorship of Kay Muhr and Nollaig Ó Muraile.

For textually-based studies of place-names (i.e. the study of placenames within an early text), we are still largely dependent on the work of the great nineteenth and early twentieth scholars such as John O'Donovan and Edmund Hogan, though an updated version of the latter's *Onomasticon Goedelicum* of 1910 is currently being developed in University College Cork. The problem for the modern scholar is that these early workers, although possessing extremely detailed knowledge of the early sources, were active in a period prior to the development of modern onomastic methodology and they tended to work on an ad hoc basis, linking an early attestation of a placename with a modern unit, without always following the identification through time in any systematic way. This tendency is still apparent in more recent works on Patrician placenames as, for example, in the identifications proffered by Éamonn de hÓir in Bieler's 1979 edition, or the 1981 UCD MPhil thesis on Tírechán's place-names by Anne-Marie Cawley.

Another hurdle in the investigation of the place-names in our list is the fact that their form and spelling, as already mentioned, belongs to the period in the development of the Irish language which is termed Early Old Irish. Both the grammar and the spelling of Irish have changed considerably since that date and it is important that we are able to identify these changes if we are to follow the attestations of a particular name or place-name through time. For example, Tírechán refers, in a list of bishops accompanying Patrick to Ireland, to a man whose name is spelt Cennannus; it is only if we know that ē in Early Old

Irish later becomes 'ía', that we can make the identification between this man and Bishop Cíanán of Duleek.[10]

Despite the difficulties, it is imperative that we attempt to define these placenames for I would argue that the format of the Mag mBreg list indicates that it is likely to represent a source used by Tírechán. Since the language indicates that it is not obviously earlier in date than Tírechán himself, I would suggest that this is the work, if not of Tírechán's foster-father Ultán, then of somebody closely contemporary with him. As an excerpt, therefore, it represents our earliest account of the Patrician churches in the area of Mag mBreg and provides us with our first description of the cult within the countryside of North Dublin and Meath from some time earlier than the 670s AD.

The first church in the Mag mBreg list is that of *Cul Mine*. Bieler, in his edition of the text, believed this to be the Latin word *culmen* in the ablative case '*culmine*' and translated it 'hilltop'. This seems to me rather unlikely, especially as we have an attested placename *Culmine* for an estate of St Mary's abbey, whose history can be traced from a Norman charter (prior to AD 1186) up to the modern townland of Coolmine in the parish of Clonsilla, Co. Dublin. If Bieler were right, this would be the only known case of a purely Latin townland name in Ireland. Instead, I would suggest that this place-name is made up of two Irish elements: *cúl* meaning back or rear and *mín* meaning arable or fertile land. (The meaning of *Culmine* would thus be 'at the back of arable land'.) Both these elements are used commonly of land units; one has only to think of the many Irish place-names beginning with 'Cool-' in English.

The second church is that of *Cerne* in which Erc is buried. Tírechán provides us with the word in its genitival form, ending in -e, and this, together with forms in other texts, suggests an -iā stem noun also ending in -e in the nominative. In the Middle Irish period, however, final vowels were often confused and it seems, therefore, that one can link this site with the *síd Cherna* 'the Otherworld mound of *Cerne*' in the Annals of Ulster under the year 868. The same site occurs in the saga text 'The

10 *Liber Ardmachanus* f.9vb 26. For further discussion of St Cíanán, see Ailbhe Mac Shamhráin's paper in this volume.

Destruction of Da Derga's hostel' in which Cormac king of Ireland came to grief through hunting the crooked beasts of *Cerne*. In the *Metrical Dindshenchus*, the site of *Cnoc Cerna* (the hill of Cerna) is said to hold the bodies of the sons and grandsons of Áed Sláine – Áed of Slane – who is remembered as king of Tara between AD 598 and 604. The Slane connection is reinforced by the fact that the Erc who died of plague in our Mag mBreg list is identified as Erc 'whose relics are worshiped in Slane' by Muirchú whose life of Patrick is also found in the Book of Armagh.[11]

There are three possible candidates for the modern location of this site. Working from Irish language sources of all periods, Eugene O'Curry suggested that Cerna is probably preserved in the townlands of Carnes East and West in the parish of Duleek.[12] Alternatively, there is a church-site listed in a fourteenth-century charter as 'Donaghkerny' which today is the modern townland of Donacarney in the parish of Colp. There is also a reference in the martryologies to *Domnach Ceirne*, which is recorded as the fifteenth-century estate of 'Donagh Kerny' near Dublin in the Register of All Hallows. Today this estate is known as Donnycarney, located between Artane and Drumcondra in north Dublin. These last two examples incorporate an early word for church, *domnach*, and both show the initial 'e' which perhaps, makes them stronger candidates than O'Curry's 'Carnes'. On the other hand, the 'ey' ending of the Anglicized name does not appear to accord with our 'a' in Cerna and moreover both the Colp and Dublin sites are low-lying rather than on a hill. In addition, the Dublin site, in particular, is a long way from Slane and the heartland of the kingdom of Áed Sláne's descendants. I would suggest that on the whole, the evidence supports O'Curry and *Cerna* should be seen as being located at the western end of Bellewstown ridge and to the south of Duleek.

The third church is in the hills of *Ais-*. This is a place which Medb's army passed as they travelled from Connacht to the Cooley peninsula at the beginning of the Táin. The poem on Sliabh Fuait (the Fews) in the *Metrical Dindshenchas* refers to the site of *Ard Asse* – the height of *Ais* –

11 *Liber Ardmachanus* 4rb 13–16. 12 E. O'Curry, *Cath Mhuige Lena or 'The battle of Magh Leana'* (Dublin, 1855), 66.

from which great views could be obtained over Louth and Armagh. From the early fourteenth century, we have reference to the manor of 'Ays' which appears to be located south-west of Dundalk around Mount Ash (on the road to Carrickmacross). This is one possible candidate for our site of *Ais-* but it seems very far to the north to be part of Mag mBreg. Furthermore, Mount Ash is only a small drumlin and Tírechán specifies hills in the plural. I would suggest instead Mullaghash in south Louth – *mullach* being another word for hill – the northern-most peak in a range of hills immediately to the north of Collon. This hill is marked as having a prehistoric barrow on its summit on the Discovery Series map, no. 36.

Our fourth church *i mBlaitiniu* poses something of a conundrum. It is normally taken to be the townland of Platin, in the parish of Duleek, immediately to the north of our chosen site for church no. 2 at Carnes. The earliest reference which I have been able to trace to this townland is in an early thirteenth-century charter where a chapel belonging to Duleek is located at 'Platyn' but there is no obvious reason why a word begining with B in Irish should become a word beginning with P in English. Furthermore, the geographical logic of the list is difficult to ascertain if churches 1 to 3 are, as I have suggested, to be located at Coolmine, Carnes?/Donnycarney? and Mullaghash. Such a distribution forms a more or less south-north trajectory but locating no. 4 at Platin would mean an abrupt return south, almost doubling back on one's self.

Church no. 5 in our list also poses problems. It is written in the Book of Armagh as *Collumb* ₃ and the scribe of the Book of Armagh indicates in the margin that he has no idea what the abbreviation ₃ signifies. Nor do we have any traditions about holy Eugenius to help us locate the church. One possible indication of *Collumb's* ₃ location is provided by an entry in the Annals of Ulster under the year 884 which refers to a leader of the *Gailenga Collumrach*. (*Mb* was often confused with *mm* in Old Irish). The epithet of this group of *Gailenga* suggests a link with the location identified in twelfth-century and later sources as the birthplace of the Ulster warrior Caoilte mac Rónáin, *Collamair Breagh* – Collamair in Mag mBreg. We know from other texts that the main branch of the Gailenga in Meath gave their name to the barony of Morgallion in the north of the county but whether the Gailenga Collumrach were located in their vicinity is not clear. Other early references to *Collamair* include the account of *Síd Collomrach* or 'Otherworld mound of *Collamair*' which is described as the home of a herd of magical pigs and the name of a mythical early king of Tara known as Conall Collumrach 'Conall of *Collamair*'. Finally, the *Acallamh Bec* tells us that *Collamair* lay between the estuary of the river Nanny, (at Laytown) and *Tuirbhe* thought to be Turvey, to the west of Donabate. Unfortunately, I have not, as yet, been able to trace any citation to *Collamair* in the post-Norman documentation. None of this is particularly satisfactory; it is possible that our fifth church lies somewhere in the area between Turvey and Laytown, but the evidence is not compelling.

Church no. 6, in contrast, is relatively well documented despite the fact that Tírechán only gives us the name of the local founder, *filius Lathphe*. In the Martyrology of Tallaght, this saint's day is identified as 20 May and he is said to be based at *Domnach Mór* whilst in the corpus of saints' genealogies in the Book of Leinster he is identified as Bishop Eithern mac Laithbe, a member of the Mugdorna. (For the observant who have noticed the two spellings of this man's name, '*ph*' can be written as '*b*' in Old Irish but only when '*b*' is in the middle of the word; the two spellings here do not negate the arguments about *Blaitine*/Platyn above.) Another martryology, the Martyrology of Gorman, states that Eithern's church lay within Mugdorna lands. We know that the Mugdorna Breg are located in the north of Co. Meath while an entry in the Annals of the Four Masters in 1150 associates *Domnach Mór mic Laithphe* with the area of the Boyne river between Slane and Navan. All of this makes it fairly certain that this is the 'Donoughmore' church recorded in the early fourteenth century, a site which later became the modern parish of Donaghmore, just outside Navan on the Slane road. The foundation is the only one in our list which shows material evidence of its medieval origins for it contains a round tower and a ruined church building.

With church no. 7, we return to confusion and poor records. *Brí Dam* – 'hill of oxen' – is recorded in the Metrical Dindshenchas as containing some of the best land in Mag mBreg while an entry in the Annals of Ulster under the year 603 refers to the killing of an Uí Néill leader by Áed Sláine at *Brí Dam* by a river. There is also a tradition in a tenth-century life of Patrick that *Brí Dam* was under the control of the Uí

Failgi but such a location (in the area of north Kildare stretching into Offaly) would seem to be outside the area of both Mag mBreg and the kingdom of Áed Sláine's descendants. It seems, in fact, that there may be two sites known as *Brí dam* for this Kildare/Offaly location is also suggested by the description of a prehistoric battle between two sons of *Míl* at *Brí Dam*, otherwise known as the battle of Geisill or Geashil parish in modern Offaly. The *Brí Dam* of Mag mBreg, meanwhile, remains unidentified.[13] Turning to the associated saints, we have no traces of the Dulcis whom Tírechán locates at this church site although Tírechán identifies his brother, Carthacus, as a bishop. Bishops named *Carthach* also occur in the genealogies and martyrologies but no geographical specification is provided.

Our final site is the church of Argetbor. The exact status of the last entry is ambiguous for it leads directly into an account of the first Easter which was celebrated in Ireland, which in both Tírechán and Muirchú's writings, is said to have taken place in Mag mBreg. The Argetbor reference is also the only entry in the Mag mBreg list to use the preposition 'above' (*super* in the original Latin) – although *super* is common in the other long list of church sites on folio 11 dealing with churches on the Meath/Westmeath border. Whether Argetbor originally formed part of the Mag mBreg list, or whether it is simply another tale which is being dovetailed into the numbered format used in this section, is not clear. It may be worth noting at this point, the use of the letter K in the bishop's name 'Kannanus'; this is an relatively rare rendition of a 'C' sound in Irish orthography and serves further to distinguish this particular sentence. (Tírechán does not use 'K' anywhere else in his text.)

The name 'Cannanus' (substituting the more normal C for K) might perhaps represent *Cainén*. *Cainén* is listed in Irish sources as a grandson or great-grandson of Shem son of Noah and this would appear to be a confused reference to the figure identified in Genesis 9:18 as Canaan son of Ham. No example of *Cainén* being used of Irish figures has been traced although the related names *Cainnech* and *Cainne* do appear. It is

---

13 Eoin MacNeill suggested that Brí Dam became St Doolagh's in Malahide on the basis that the dedication may be a reflex of the name Dulcis, see his article 'The Vita Tripartita of St Patrick', *Ériu*, 11 (1932), 1–41, 40–1. However, I can see no obvious relationship between the two names and I don't find the suggestion convincing.

possible therefore, that the bishop of Argetbor is named after an Irish version of a Hebrew name (which has subsequently been given the Latin ending *-us*). Alternatively, if we assume that Tírechán's 'Kannanus' with an 'a' is a mistaken spelling for Cennanus with a 'e', the hero of this anecdote would be the well-known Cíanán of Duleek. (As mentioned above, ē in Early Old Irish later becomes ía.) It is, of course, somewhat self-serving to amend our only existing text in this way; the only justification one could proffer is that it would mean that a well-known Patrician saint had an important role in the story of the first Easter as Tírechán describes it. If we do not amend in this fashion, we must assume that this important figure was completely obliterated in later traditions of the Patrician cult.

There are no known records of Argetbor in the place-name sources of either pre-Norman or post-Norman date. *Fertae Fer Féicc* (the 'Burial-mound of the men of Fíacc') is identified by both Tírechán and his contemporary Muirchú as the location for the celebration of the first Easter, although only Tírechán refers to the presence of Bishop 'Kannanus'. The *fertae* has normally in the past been taken to be the hill of Slane, but I have argued elsewhere that this ignores at least one early legal gloss which states that the *fertae* was south of the River Boyne.[14] If we assume that the name is really 'Cennanus' i.e. Cíanán, the most prominent site associated with the latter is of course Duleek. There is, however, also a church known as *Cell Cíanáin* 'the church of Cíanán' on the northern bank of the Boyne, to the east of Monasterboice. This, too, could conceivably be the site of Argetbor. I have not been able to trace this last placename in the post-Norman records.

What then can we conclude from this rather inconclusive investigation of the placenames in the Mag mBreg list? Of the list of eight churches, only that of the sixth church, belonging to the son of Laithphe, appears secure whilst the arguments for each of the others are problematic in various degrees. Following the identifications proposed here, the list produces a sequence which runs as follows:

14 C. Swift, 'Pagan monuments and Christian legal centres in early Meath', *Ríocht na Midhe*, 9 no. 2 (1996), 1–27, 10–11; see also K. Hollo, 'Cú Chulainn and Síd Truim', *Ériu*, 49 (1998), 13–23 for a contrary view.

No. 1   Coolmine, Clonsilla, Co. Dublin
No. 2   Carnes East & West, Duleek, Co. Meath (or Donnycarney, Co.
         Dublin or Donacarney, Colp, Co. Meath)
No. 3   Mullaghash, Mosstown, Co. Louth
No. 4   Platin, Duleek, Co. Meath
No. 5?   *Collamair*, somewhere between Laytown and Turvey, Co. Dublin
No. 6   Donaghmore, Co. Meath (outside Navan)
No. 7?   *Brí Dam* – unlocated.
No. 8?   possibly Duleek, Co. Meath, possibly *Cell Cíannan* east of
         Monasterboice, Co. Louth

If this diverse group includes correct identifications, we are left with a
series of churches which are arranged in no obvious geographical order
whilst up to three candidates may possibly have been located within the
parish of Duleek. What this means is not clear but may imply an early
association between Patrick's church and the cult of Cíanán. There is also
an apparent association with the figure of Áed Sláine or Áed of Slane for his
descendants were buried at *Cnoc Cerna* whilst he himself killed another
dynast at *Brí Dam*. This connection is visible elsewhere in the early evidence for Patrick's cult which seems to have been patronised in the seventh
century by the kings of Síl nÁedo Sláine or descendants of Áed of Slane.[15]

Five of the eight churches appear to be concentrated in the eastern
half of Brega, a concentration which would agree with the important
role given to Skerries as the site chosen for Patrick's arrival in Ireland as
a missionary. If this Mag mBreg list is an excerpt from Ultán's book, it
seems odd that such a focus lies at some distance from the area of Ultán's
church at Ardbraccan, to the west of Navan. (Only church no. 6, at
Donaghmore, seems to be sited in the general vicinity of Ardbraccan).
In any event, the list would seem to imply a relatively widespread cult of
Patrick in eastern Brega sometime before the middle of the seventh
century AD.

Given the poor quality of the evidence we are dealing with, these
interpretations can only be put forward very tentatively and further work

---

15 See C. Swift, 'Tírechán's motives in compiling the *Collectanea*: an alternative interpretation',
Ériu, 45 (1994), 53–85.

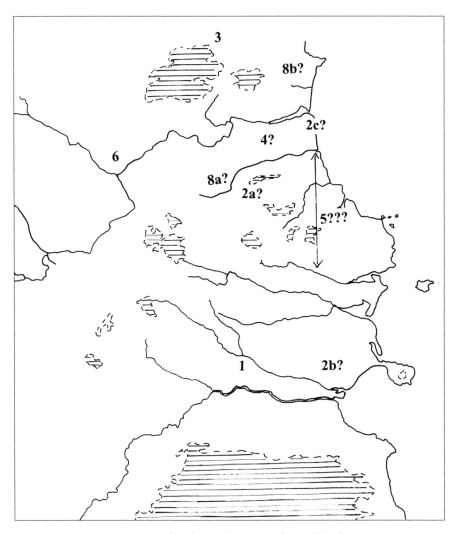

4.1 Patrician churches in Brega according to Tírechán

Location of possible sites of churches listed in the Brega extract incorporated into Tírechán's seventh-century *Collectanae*. 1: Coolmine; 2a: Carnes East & West; 2b: Donnycarney; 2c: Donacarney; 3: Mullaghash; 4: Platin; 5: *Collamair* between Laytown and Turvey; 6: Donaghmore; 7: *Brí Dam* – unlocated; 8a: Duleek; 8b *Cell Ciannain*

on the post-Norman sources of Counties Meath and Dublin is required to try and pin down the location of sites such as *Brí Dam* or *Argetbor*. Even if the investigations to date have not brought forward secure identifications, however, the pre-Norman references have highlighted certain characteristics of these churches which were not indicated explicitly by Tírechán. The first of these, as already suggested, is the emphasis on bishops. The Mag mBreg list tells us that both holy Eugenius and 'Cannanus' were bishops whilst elsewhere Tírechán specifies that Dulcis' brother Carthacus also held episcopal rank. The genealogies indicate that Eithern mac Laithbe of Donaghmore also belonged to this category. If we can assume that the Erc who lay buried at *aeclessia Cerne* is to be linked to Erc mac Dego, whose relics were kept at Slane, then he too is stated in the genealogies to have been a bishop. We know nothing of the patron saint of *Ais-* or of *Cul míne* and although the martryologies tell us that a saint Tigernach was linked to Blaitine, we know nothing further about him. Thus five of our eight churches are given the highest possible clerical rank which tells us something of the status of the Patrician churches at this time. Futhermore, the emphasis on high-ranking clerics can be compared with the description of Patrick's arrival in Skerries where the saint is said to have been accompanied by clerics of all ranks. At no stage are abbots or monks mentioned. The exorcists, door-keepers, readers and young boys who were also part of Patrick's retinue would not be seen as functionaries in the modern church, but in the middle ages these were all categorised as junior ranks within the clergy.

The second element to emerge from a study of the placenames is the emphasis on height. *Ais-* is identified explicitly with hills in the Mag mBreg list whilst the placename *Brí Dam* means hill of oxen. *Cerna* is identified as *Cnoc Cerna* or hill of Cerna in the Metrical Dindshenchas and has been associated here with Bellewstown ridge. Platin is in an area of small hills whilst Donaghmore is on the lower slopes of a low ridge running along the northern edge of the Boyne. Coolmine is on the southern edge of a low ridge overlooking the Tolka river. The exception here is Duleek (if indeed, Argetbor is Duleek) which lies in the valley of the river Nanny.

A third feature is association with Otherworld mounds or '*síde*'. Both *Cerna* and *Collamair* are explicitly identified as *síd Cerna* and *síd*

Collumrach respectively. The type of burial mound known as a *fertae* is often identified as the location for encounters with Otherworldly figures such as the Túatha Dé Danann and *Fertae Fer Féicc* is identified in Patrician tradition not only as the scene of the first Easter but also as a mound commemorated by one of the most famous druids of Mag mBreg. *Blaitine* and *Brí Dam* are both identified as *dindgnai* or monuments of Ireland in a poem on Tara whilst a prehistoric barrow is located on the summit of Mullaghash. Again Duleek proves the exception although one should note the presence of another barrow to the south of the town in the townland of Abbeyland.

An emphasis on heights and on Otherworldly mounds would seem to run counter to the identification of these churches with bishops, for bishops are primarily the religious leaders of lay communities and settlements and we might expect to find their churches in areas of habitation. At least some of these Patrician churches in Mag mBreg, in contrast, appear to lie outside settlements and to be associated with monuments connected with pre-Christian Irish beliefs. If so, our list may provide insights into the function of churches founded by the early followers of Patrick. In the year 601, Pope Gregory sent instructions to Bishop Augustine, leader of the English mission to convert the Anglo-Saxons:

> the idol temples of the English should by no means be destroyed but only idols in them. Take holy water and sprinkle it in the shrines, build altars and place relics in them. For if the shrines are well built, it is essential that they should be changed from the worship of devils to the service of the true God. When these people see that their shrines are not destroyed, they will be able to banish error from their hearts and be more ready to come to the places they are familiar with but now recognising and worshipping the true God.[16]

The churches of the Mag mBreg list indicate that some time before the 670s, high-ranking Irish clerics were credited with having founded churches of the type called for by Gregory in England. A minimum of

---

16 *Bede's Ecclesiastical history of the English people*, ed. B. Colgrave & R.A.B. Mynors (Oxford, 1969), i, 30.

two of the churches described here are named as Otherworld mounds or *síde* – which, in pagan Irish belief, were locations where humans were most likely to encounter Otherworld beings. These churches form part of a group of sites, apparently focussed in the east of Mag mBreg, which provide us with the earliest known traditions of Patrick's cult. These churches tended to be situated on hill-sites, apparently at some distance from arable land although the saints with whom these churches were associated were predominantly bishops. At least two of the church sites were linked to the ancestor of the Síl nÁedo Sláine, the most powerful kingdom in Mag mBreg in the seventh century. (One site, indeed, is identified as the royal burial ground.) Tírechán describes Patrick's arrival at Skerries 'at sunrise … lighting the thick clouds of ignorance', and in relation to the local history of Patrick's cult in the middle ages, we are still lamentably ignorant for most studies to date have focussed on the saint's national role rather than his regional importance. The Skerries community have done great service to us all by focussing our minds on the local history of Patrick. In this regard, Tírechán's *Collectanea* is not only of importance in locating Patrick's arrival into Ireland at Skerries but also in providing us with evidence for the role and importance of Patrick's cult in the general area during the seventh century – the earliest account of local church organization to be found anywhere in Ireland.

Peregrinatio Columbae

CORMAC BOURKE

God's instruction to Abraham[1] prefaces the twelfth-century, Middle Irish life of Columba (obit *c*.597)[2] in two languages and signals the saint's status as emigrant *par excellence*:

> *Exi de terra tua et de cognatione tua et de domo patris tui et vade in terram quam tibi monstravero. Facaib do thir 7 do thalmain, do choibnes collaide 7 t'athardu ndiles erumsa 7 eirg isin tir faillsigfet-sa duit.*
> 'Leave your country and your land, your kindred and your patrimony for my sake, and go into the country which I shall reveal to you.'[3]

The life written or compiled by Maghnas Ó Domhnaill in 1532 is more explicit.[4] Columba is once again likened to Abraham;[5] there is reference to his 'separation from the Irish', *delughadh re Gaidhealaibh*,[6] and to his 'exile', *deoraidhecht*, in 'foreign distant lands', *tírtha ciana comhaighecha*.[7] Scholarship has acquiesced in this portrait. Thus Charles-Edwards, speaking of the lesser and higher grades of *peregrinatio*, or self-expatriation for one's soul's sake, cites Columba as an example of the latter, intensive form.[8] The distinction is set out in the life of Columbanus (obit 615) written *c*.640 by Jonas, a Continental-born monk of Bobbio. He speaks of a nun who had moved within Ireland to her 'place of pilgrimage',

---

1 Genesis 12:1. **2** Cited as *ILCC: The Irish Life of Colum Cille*, ed. & trans. M. Herbert, in M. Herbert, *Iona, Kells, and Derry: the history and hagiography of the monastic Familia of Columba* (Oxford, 1988; repr. Dublin, 1996), 209–88. **3** *ILCC* § 1. **4** Cited as *BCC*: A O'Kelleher & G Schoepperle (ed. & trans.), *Betha Colaim Chille, Life of Columcille* (Urbana, 1918; repr. Dublin, 1994), in citing which I have sometimes adjusted the translation. See also B. Lacey (trans.), *The Life of Colum Cille by Manus O'Donnell* (Dublin, 1998). **5** *BCC* § 378. **6** *BCC* § 189. **7** *BCC* §§ 190, 196, 378. *ILCC* anticipates, referring once to *tirtha ciana comaithecha* (§ 10, with n 101), although with less specific allusion to Columba's experience. **8** T.M. Charles-Edwards, 'The social background to Irish *peregrinatio*', *Celtica*, 11 (1976), 43–59, at 44; repr. in J. Wooding (ed.), *The otherworld voyage in early Irish literature: an anthology of criticism* (Dublin, 2000), 94–108; see also Herbert, *Iona, Kells, and Derry*, 28.

peregrinationis locus; had she not been a woman, she would, 'having crossed the sea', *mare transacto,* have sought a 'place of greater pilgrimage', *potioris peregrinationis locus.*⁹ Columbanus achieved both grades of pilgrimage, moving from Leinster to Ulster and, ultimately, mainland Europe. But the requirement to travel 'overseas' reflects a Continental perspective, and Jonas can scarcely have appreciated insular geography. A *potior peregrinatio* might indeed be achieved by travelling overseas, but it depended on which seas. Thus while Columba is portrayed by tradition as archetypal exile, his was not, as I hope to show, a *potior peregrinatio*; he remained among the Irish in the Irish-speaking world.¹⁰

The chief source for our enquiry is the Latin life of Columba written about a century after his death by the ninth abbot of Iona, Adomnán (obit 704).¹¹ Adomnán belonged, like Columba, to the Cenél Conaill of Co. Donegal, but lived and wrote in the monastery of Iona in the Inner Hebrides which Columba had founded *c.*563. In his First Preface Adomnán sets out his terms of reference, asking his readers' indulgence for his use of names in the Irish language, 'words that, I suppose, are held to be of no value, among other different tongues of foreign peoples',

9 *Passiones Vitaeque Sanctorum Aevi Merovingici,* ed. B. Krusch (*Monumenta Germaniae Historica, Scriptorum Rerum Merovingicarum* 4) (Leipzig/Hannover, 1902), 68. **10** Charles-Edwards, modifying his view of Columba's *peregrinatio,* has more recently suggested that although he left Ireland for Britain, Columba 'remained within the Irish people' and 'had not left the Irish': *Early Christian Ireland* (Cambridge, 2000), 284, 293. I take the point made by Thomas Clancy (pers. comm.) that the Irish might be termed 'Gaels' in this discussion, and so associated with Ireland and Scotland without qualification. But I adhere to the former term, and am mindful of the observation made by G.A. Hayes-McCoy, *Scots mercenary forces in Ireland (1565–1603)* (Dublin / London, 1937), 4–5, n. 1, that 'under the scheme of Chancellor Maitland for tightening up control over the Highlands and Isles in 1590, the Highlands were officially called "Ireland"'. By the same token Scottish Gaelic is called 'the Irish language' in M. Martin, *A description of the Western Islands of Scotland c.1695,* ed. D.J. Macleod (Stirling 1934), 102 (North Rona), 154 (South Uist), 252 (Bute), 260 (Arran), 264 (Gigha) etc. **11** Cited as *VC: Adomnan's Life of Columba,* ed. & trans. A.O. Anderson & M.O. Anderson (London, 1961; rev. edn Oxford, 1991), which is quoted here for both text and translation. See also W. Reeves (ed.), *The Life of St Columba, founder of Hy* (Dublin 1857); *Adomnán of Iona, Life of St Columba,* trans. R. Sharpe (London, 1995). It is appropriate to refer at this point to the earliest documentary witness to the cult of Columba, the Old Irish *Amra Coluim Cille,* a poetic eulogy of the saint written shortly after his death *c.*597. Although allusive and difficult of interpretation, the *Amra* seems not to refer to the nature or quality of Columba's separation. See, for text, translation and commentary, T.O. Clancy & G. Márkus, *Iona: the earliest poetry of a Celtic monastery* (Edinburgh, 1995), 96–128. Two seventh-century poems by Beccán mac Luigdech, on the other hand, characterize Columba as having crossed the sea in a spirit of self-denial: ibid., 129–63.

vocabula, quae ut puto inter alias exterarum gentium diversas vilescunt linguas. Adomnán opposes the Irish language, rhetorically, to all others, and recognizes the linguistic continuity (which was likewise religious, social and cultural) between Ireland and Scottish Dál Riata[12] in his own experience and, presumably, in that of his sainted predecessor.

Adomnán reports that Columba 'sailed away from Ireland to Britain, wishing to be a pilgrim for Christ', *de Scotia ad Brittanniam pro Christo perigrinari volens enavigavit.*[13] Ireland and Britain are perceived to be separate islands, even though, as we shall see, the distinction can be blurred in Adomnán's mind. But allowing the distinction, Columba is not represented as an exile from Ireland in terms of modern convention. For Adomnán, and doubtless for Columba, what mattered was *patria*, the home place, the equivalent (as the twelfth-century life attests)[14] of Irish *atharda*. This is not Ireland in Adomnán's usage, but the specific *part* of Ireland from which an individual hails. The distinction is clear in his account of Librán who, having sailed from Ireland to Iona, is quizzed by the saint as to his 'country, his family and the cause of his journey', *de patria de gente et causa iteneris.*[15] Similarly Oengus, driven from his country, *de patria*, is the subject of a favourable prophecy by Columba.[16] He will eventually reign, we read, in his country, *in patria*, in allusion not to Ireland but to the lands of the Cenél Coirpri Gabra in Co. Longford.[17]

The example which is most revealing of Adomnán's thinking concerns not a human traveller but a bird.[18] The famous heron which lands exhausted on Iona after a direct flight from Ireland is welcomed by Columba not because it comes from Ireland, but because it comes from 'the northern region of Ireland', *aquilonalis Everniae regio*, from that 'sweet district of Ireland', *Scotiae dulcis regio*, from 'the district of our fathers', *nostrae paternitatis regio.*[19] The bird is best interpreted as

---

12 As distinct from Irish Dál Riata in Co. Antrim; the designations 'Scottish' and 'Irish' are unhelpful, as will appear, but such is the established terminology. **13** *VC*, Second Preface. It is worth noting that the verb *enavigare* carries no special connotation; it is used again with reference to Columba's first journey from Ireland to Iona in *VC* i. 7, but in ii. 15 refers to journeys from Iona to Ireland and from Iona to nearby Tiree. Cf. J.E. Rekdal, who takes *enavigare* to suggest the idea of a quest: 'The Irish ideal of pilgrimage as reflected in the tradition of Colum Cille (Columba)', in A. Ó Corráin (ed.), *Proceedings of the Third Symposium of Societas Celtologica Nordica held in Oslo, 1–2 November 1991* (*Studia Celtica Upsaliensia* 1), (Uppsala 1994), 67–83, at 76. **14** *ILCC* § 6, 8. **15** *VC* ii. 39. **16** *VC* i. 13. **17** Sharpe, *Adomnán of Iona*, n 94. **18** *VC* i. 48. **19** In *VC* i. 35 *regio, dioecesis* and *patria* are

allegorical of the saint;[20] Adomnán calls it pilgrim, *perigrina*, and its journey a pilgrimage, *perigrinatio*, no doubt consciously echoing the terms which, he gives us to believe, Columba had used of himself.[21] The heron's journey retraces the saint's own, but its early return to its *patria* underlines his continuing separation.[22] The same story, retold by Ó Domhnaill in 1532, betrays a focal shift: the place of the bird's origin is said to be Ireland and is not more precisely defined.[23] While the monk who tends the heron hails from the same 'patrimony and land', *duthaigh 7 … talmhain*, these terms are more bland than they seem. Only Ireland is referred to, or so I conclude from the closing observation, following the heron's departure for *Ireland*, that Columba loved not only the people but also the wild creatures of 'his native land', *a thír duthaighe fen*.[24]

Columba is a pilgrim, *perigrinus*, but his separation, for Adomnán, is of his own choice, what the twelfth-century life calls 'voluntary pilgrimage', *oilithre toltanach*.[25] The opposite experience, located firmly

---

equivalents.   **20** J.F. Nagy, *Conversing with angels and ancients: literary myths of medieval Ireland* (Dublin, 1997), 184–5; G. Márkus, 'Iona: monks, pastors and missionaries', in D. Broun & T.O. Clancy (ed.), *Spes Scotorum: hope of Scots* (Edinburgh 1999), 115–38, at 115–16. **21** *VC* iii. 22.   **22** Adomnán is being geographically precise in implying a *direct* flight from the lands of the Cenél Conaill to Iona. There is no landfall between the two, unless Inishtrahull, Co. Donegal, six miles north-east of Malin Head (which was in Cenél nEógain territory), counts as such. The traverse from Derry or the Co. Antrim coast, by contrast, can take in Rathlin, Islay and/or Jura, and Colonsay. On a clear day in August 2000 I looked eastwards from Inishtrahull (Ireland's most northerly point) and saw Fair Head (Co. Antrim), Rathlin, Kintyre and Islay. Far away to the north-east the horizon was interrupted by the unexpected sight of land, and decisively interrupted, given the distance evidently involved. Was it Ben More (3171 ft), the massy mountain on Mull which overlooks Iona from the east? The distance would be 85 miles as the heron flies, and D.D.C. Pochin Mould, *Scotland of the saints* (London, 1952), 164, assures us that Ireland can be seen from Ben More. In these terms, contrary to canonical belief, Ireland and Iona are intervisible.   **23** *BCC* § 265.   **24** That Scandlán mac Colmáin's home kingdom of Osraige is similarly referred to as his *tir duthaigh* (*BCC* § 348) must be read in context and does not bear on the manner of Columba's characterization. Ó Domhnaill also refers (*BCC* § 127) to the expulsion of the Irish to the marginal lands of Ireland from 'their own heritage and patrimony', *as a ndutchus 7 as a n-athardha fen*.   **25** *ILCC* § 10. For the association between Columba's separation and the battle of Cúl Drebene see the tract *De causa peregrinationis S. Columbae*, in H.J. Lawlor, 'The Cathach of St Columba', *RIA Proc.*, 33 C (1900), 241–443, at 408–12; Herbert, *Iona, Kells, and Derry*, 27–8; Sharpe, *Adomnán of Iona*, 12–14; Rekdal, 'The Irish ideal of pilgrimage', 73–4, 77–9. Charles-Edwards, *Early Christian Ireland*, 299–308, endorses the view that Columba was concerned in leaving Ireland to evangelize the Picts. Cf my own observation that 'Columba … was forty before he left Ireland, and it may be that his career should be seen in terms of a progressive distancing from his native heath, the better to answer his monastic calling. The

by Adomnán in secular society, is that of the *exsul*, the man banished or forced into exile against his will. Oengus, already mentioned, is one such.[26] Evidently ejected in a succession dispute, Oengus comes to Columba in Iona. The difference between them is tellingly expressed by Adomnán: 'this man, driven out from his country ... , came as an exile to Britain, to the saint living in pilgrimage there', *hic namque de patria ... effugatus, ad sanctum in Britanniam perigrinantem exsul venit*. In Adomnán's terms one is *perigrinus*, the other *exsul*.[27] Likewise Tarain, 'of a noble family of the Picts' (in Scotland), and committed to Columba's care, is termed *exsul*, doubtless because his separation was involuntary.[28] Oswald, future king of Northumbria, also spent some years through force of circumstances 'in exile among the Irish' (in Scotland), *Scotos inter exsolans*.[29] The same terminology is used again by Adomnán of Scandlán, of the royal family of Osraige, who was a hostage in 'exile', *exsilium*, among the Cenél Conaill and who, after becoming king, 'was [again] in exile for some period of time', *per aliquod exsolavit spatium temporis*.[30]

Adomnán identifies another potential *exsul*, although he avoids this fate only to meet another, in the person of an unnamed man who comes to Iona (presumably from Ireland) and who, Columba divines, has committed fratricide and incest.[31] The saint's judgment, which the man professes to accept, is that he should do penance 'among the Britons', *inter Brittones*, 'with wailing and weeping', *cum fletu et lacrimis*, for twelve years and never return to Ireland, *Scotia*, as long as he lives.[32] This is a punishment ostensibly of two phases: the first is the equivalent of

---

monastic ideal is not to be underestimated, and that the personnel of Iona came to include Irishmen, Britons, Anglo-Saxons and, in all likelihood, Picts may be more than an accident of location, and such fraternity might well have been planned. Viewed in this light, Columba's yearning to be a 'pilgrim for Christ' takes second place, despite Adomnán, and becomes the corollary of his primary motivation': C. Bourke, 'A view of the early Irish church', in A.-C. Larsen (ed. & trans.) *The Vikings in Ireland* (Roskilde, 2001), 77–86, at 80. **26** *VC* i.13. **27** The seventh-century penitential of Cummean uses *exul (sic)* of a cleric in penitential exile: L Bieler (ed.), *The Irish penitentials* (Dublin, 1963; repr 1975), 114–15 § 17. An Irishman on the Continent in the eight century styles himself (as Thomas Clancy has pointed out to me) *Hibernicus exul*: J.F. Kenney, *The sources for the early history of Ireland: ecclesiastical* (New York, 1929; repr. Shannon, 1968), 541; and Boniface, the Anglo-Saxon apostle to the Germans, calls himself *exul Germanicus*: K. Hughes, 'The changing theory and practice of Irish pilgrimage', *Jnl. Ecclesiastical Hist.*, 11 (1960), 143–51, at 145 (repr. in K. Hughes, *Church and society in Ireland*, AD 400–1200, ed. D. Dumville (London 1987), Chapter xiv). **28** *VC* ii. 23. **29** *VC* i.1. **30** *VC* i.11. **31** *VC* i.22. **32** Here I follow the translation of Sharpe, *Adomnán of Iona*.

potior peregrinatio which, as I argue, was not Columba's own experience; the second, to begin at the end of twelve years, might be lesser *peregrinatio* such as Columba knew. Understood in these terms, it must be allowed that a man guilty of fratricide and incest can hope for readmission to the *loci sancti* of Iona although barred forever from Ireland itself. But Columba tries to preserve Iona from the contamination of the man's presence, just as he tries to preserve Ireland in perpetuity. Moreover the sentence is imposed by one Irishman on another and, because handed down on Iona, has yet to begin, so that 'Ireland', *Scotia*, for the purposes of its imposition seems to embrace Iona and the Irish-speaking world.[33] Thus the second phase of the sentence must be understood to refer to a period (the rest of the man's life) spent other than in penance 'with wailing and weeping' but outside the Irish-speaking world and in continuing *potior peregrinatio*. That the man rejects Columba's judgment by returning to Ireland need not be fatal to this interpretation, albeit that it exposes an ambiguity, and can be read in baldly factual terms. He is soon killed, we learn, by the Fir Lí, but belonged to the neighbouring Uí Thuirtri and had evidently gone home to his *patria*.

The sentence passed on the miscreant Irishman is realized in reverse, one assumes voluntarily, in the case of the British monk in Iona whom Adomnán mentions but coincidentally fails to name.[34] This man is taken by Charles-Edwards to exemplify lesser *peregrinatio*, seemingly on the grounds that he has not gone 'overseas' and remains, technically, in *Brittannia*.[35] But he has left his kin-group, his society and his fellow British-speakers and shares, in terms of degree, the experience of the Anglo-Saxon prince Oswald when he lived *Scotos inter exsolans*. Charles-Edwards equates

---

33 *Scotia* is otherwise distinct from *Brittannia* (including Iona) in Adomnán's Second Preface and in iii. 22, with reference to Columba's separation. *Scotia* and *Ebernia / Evernia* are equivalents in i. 2 (Fintan), i. 12 (sailors), i. 17 (Colcu) and i. 48 (heron). The Irish themselves, by contrast, are *Scoti* but never *Hibernenses*, *Hiberionaci* or *Hibernici*. Adomnán might have avoided the latter terms, given that the party favouring the 'Celtic' Easter (which included the Iona community, with the exception of Adomnán) called themselves *Hibernenses*. The *Liber Angeli*, by contrast, uses *Scoti* and *Hibernenses* as equivalents: L. Bieler (ed. & trans.), *The Patrician Texts in the Book of Armagh* (Dublin 1979), 188–9 § 27. This Armagh document is dated to shortly after 678 by Charles-Edwards, *Early Christian Ireland*, 438–9, and so is contemporary with Adomnán; it may be significant that Armagh had by now conformed to the Roman Easter. **34** *VC* iii. 6. **35** Charles-Edwards, 'Social background', 44. Plummer argued that, for Bede, Iona belonged to *Scotia* rather than *Brittannia*: *Venerabilis Baedae Opera Historica*, ed. C. Plummer 2 vols., (Oxford 1896), ii, 186.

those engaging in *peregrinatio* and *potior peregrinatio* respectively with the *ambue* and the *cú glas* of Irish vernacular tradition. He observes that the *cú glas* 'In the typical case ... is an *Albanach*, a Briton', and goes on to cite Patrick as a classic example: 'Patrick was a Briton, an *Albanach*, and therefore a *cú glas*, a complete outsider.'[36] The Iona monk, although a less extreme case, was Patrick's compatriot and surely exemplifies *potior peregrinatio*, issues of distance notwithstanding.[37]

There is further evidence of Adomnán's thinking in two stories which he tells in succession, concerning Fintan mac Tulcháin and Ernéne mac Craséni.[38] Of Fintan, founder of Taghmon, we read that he 'was afterwards held in high repute among all the churches of the Irish', *postea per universas Scotorum eclesias valde noscibilis habetus est*. Of Ernéne, who is associated with Rathnew, Co. Wicklow,[39] Adomnán says that he was 'famous afterwards among all the churches of Ireland, and very widely known', *postea per omnes Scotiae eclesias famosus et valde notissimus*. These are parallel tributes and convey the same sense, but one mentions 'Ireland', *Scotia*, the other 'the Irish', *Scoti*. Clearly the reputations of both men extended to Columban churches *in Scotland* and, in effect, throughout the Irish-speaking world. Adomnán makes no distinction between their degrees of fame but betrays by unconscious verbal nuance that Irish ethnicity and Irish identity were more than Ireland could hold.[40]

Adomnán, incidentally, says Fintan hoped in 'leaving Ireland', *Hevernia deserens*, to live with Columba in pilgrimage, just as Columba, according to

36 'Social background', 47, 55. 37 As Charles-Edwards has pointed out, 'Social background', 55, Patrick calls himself both *peregrinus* and *proselitus*, an equivalence which recurs in Adomnan's usage (*VC* i. 32, 44). Patrick's reference to his *patria* likewise, it seems, anticipates Adomnán; in three out of five instances he couples *patria* with *parentes*. *Confessio* §§ 36, 43; *Epistola* § 1: K. Devine, *A computer-generated concordance of the Libri Epistolarum of Saint Patrick* (Dublin, 1989). Bede, as Charles-Edwards further points out, 'Social background', 45, uses *patria* to refer to Britain rather than to individual homelands within it. 38 *VC* i. 2, 3. The sequence, it has been suggested, might have arisen from the record of the deaths of both men in the same year, 635, in the 'Iona chronicle', a source incorporated in the *Annals of Ulster* which may have been available to Adomnán: A.P. Smyth, 'The earliest Irish annals: their first contemporary entries, and the earliest centres of recording', *RIA Proc.*, 72 C (1972), 1–48, at 38–40. 39 Herbert, *Iona, Kells, and Derry*, 283, n 388. 40 See n. 33 above. Ségéne, fifth abbot of Iona, was numbered without distinction among the senior Irish clergy to whom John, pope-elect, wrote a letter in 640. His letter was a *reply*, and his correspondents themselves can have made no distinction (that Ségéne must have been born in Ireland is, I think, a technicality in the context): Kenney, *The sources for the early history of Ireland*, 221–3. I note that an index of early Irish ecclesiastical sites in forty-seven pages includes Iona as the sole extra-territorial name: A. Gwynn & R.N. Hadcock, *Medieval*

his Second Preface, had sailed 'from Ireland to Britain', *de Scotia ad Brittanniam*, wishing to be a pilgrim for Christ. Both cases appear to suggest that separation from Ireland was the essence of the sacrifice, and that Ireland and *patria*, contrary to my argument, were essentially one. But, without denying the apparent sense, Adomnán's words can be read in more general than specific terms; the general, after all, embraces the specific, and Ireland included both men's *patria*. Fintan, moreover, on arriving in Iona, is questioned by Baíthíne 'as to his family and province', *de gente et provincia*, just as Columba had questioned the newly arrived Librán *de patria, de gente*. Fintan's *peregrinatio*, while it was not to be achieved in Iona, in the end conformed to type. Guided by Columba's foreknowledge, Baíthíne directs Fintan to Leinster where his true vocation lies. As a native of the north-west (adjacent to Derry, from whence he took ship),[41] Fintan was as much a stranger in Leinster as he would have been in western Scotland and so attained an equivalent *peregrinatio*.

The scope of Irish geography as intimated by Adomnán is reflected in the eighth- or ninth-century life of St Samthann of Clonbroney, Co. Longford.[42] The saint dissuades a man who wants 'to travel overseas', *transfretare*, on pilgrimage and rejects the idea that God cannot be found 'on this side of the sea', *citra mare*; because God is accessible from anywhere, Samthann says, there is no need to journey overseas. But the preceding passage tells of a boatload of wool brought from Iona to the mouth of the Boyne, as though an unremarkable occurrence, and a storm at sea is mentioned only to magnify Samthann's name. Clearly Iona belonged to the Irish world and was reckoned, despite the literal contradiction, to be *citra mare*, 'on this side of the sea'.[43] The opposite is

---

religious houses: Ireland (London, 1970), 435. **41** Sharpe, *Adomnán of Iona*, nn 53, 106; Charles Edwards, *Early Christian Ireland*, 337, n 275. **42** *Vitae Sanctorum Hiberniae*, ed. C. Plummer, (Oxford 1910; repr 1968), ii, 260 § 24. **43** Hughes, 'Changing theory and practice', 147, cites Samthann's ruling in illustration of a second phase of Irish pilgrimage, the first phase having been favourable to overseas travel. While this evolutionary pattern might be valid in broad outline, 'Ireland' must be defined in terms of the Irish-speaking world for both phases: Hughes also cites a ninth-century Tallaght commonplace book for its injunction (§ 17), attributed to Máel Ruain, that 'anyone who deserts his country (*nach oen déraich a tír*), except to go from the east to the west, and from the north to the south, is a denier of Patrick in heaven and of the faith in Ireland': E.J. Gwynn & W.J. Purton (ed. & trans.), 'The monastery of Tallaght', *RIA Proc.*, 29 C (1911–12), 115–79. But granted that *tír* refers to the individual *atharda* or *patria*, there is ambiguity as to whether travelling in the prescribed directions is permitted *inside* it or outside it within a wider frame of reference; cf the corresponding entry in J. O'Donovan (ed.

implied in the life of St Fintan of Dún Bleisce (Doon), Co. Limerick, in which Findlug (the saint's brother) is said to travel 'beyond the sea', *ultra mare*, presumably with reference to Islay (between Ireland and Iona), where Loch Finlaggan preserves his name.[44]

The terms *peregrinus* and *peregrinatio* are used by Adomnán in more senses than one, since they can refer to the individual and the individual Christian life. Columba's life, i.e. his whole lifetime, is called a 'weary pilgrimage', *tedialis perigrinatio*,[45] and the unnamed British monk at the point of death is termed *perigrinus*.[46] Paradoxically, in terms of its English derivative, the verb *emigrare* typically refers to dying in Adomnán's text, and in dying Columba will attain to the 'heavenly fatherland', *caelistis patria*.[47] In this *patria* there is oneness with the Father, as though in ultimate realization of the Irish identification with kin.

Columba's approaching death occasions a valedictory blessing in which he predicts that 'great and especial honour', *grandus et non mediocris honor*, will be bestowed on Iona 'not only [by] the kings of the Irish with their peoples, but also the rulers of barbarous and foreign nations', *non tantum Scotorum reges cum populis, sed etiam barbararum et exterarum gentium regnatores*.[48] In opposing, in this his final chapter, the

---

& trans.), 'Prose rule of the Céli Dé', in W. Reeves, *The Culdees of the British Islands* (Dublin, 1864; repr. Llanerch, 1994), 84–97, at 90–1. The wider frame need not be Ireland and might as easily be the Irish-speaking world. The former text, moreover, makes such frequent allusion to Columba, Adomnán and other Iona personnel (§§ 8, 47, 52, 65, 66, 68, 69, 80, 85) as to confirm their centrality in the Irish Christian mind. Hughes' citation of early penitentials, 'Changing theory and practice', 145, n. 6, 147, n. 7, to illustrate her first phase of pilgrimage is likewise open to question: exile from *patria* seems not to refer to *Ireland*, as Hughes assumes, but to the individual homeland, which is likewise Adomnán's usage. Thus, explicitly, Finnian prescribes that one class of offender 'be driven from *his* country', *exterminabitur de patria sua*, and beaten with rods until he repents: Bieler, *The Irish penitentials*, 84–5 § 31. **44** *Vitae Sanctorum Hiberniae, ex Codice olim Salmanticensi nunc Bruxellensi*, ed. W.W. Heist (Brussels 1965), 116; Reeves, *The Life of St Columba*, 136 (identifying this Findlug with a monk of the same name mentioned in *VC* ii. 24). Consider also the life of Colmán of Lynally, Co. Offaly, in which Colmán, departing 'into exile', *in exilium*, visits Columba in Iona. Columba advises him not to concern himself with 'other peoples', *gentes alternae*, and not to abandon his 'Irish people', *gens hybernicana*, adding that he himself had come to that quarter of necessity, *Nam ego necessitate veni in hanc regionem*: Heist, *Vitae*, 213–4. Bitel relates this account to the teaching that a churchman's first pastoral care is his *patria*, and it might have been expressly composed in illustration: L.M. Bitel, *Isle of the saints: monastic settlement and Christian community in early Ireland* (Ithaca/London, 1990), 230, n. 33; Bieler, *The Irish penitentials*, 190–1. **45** *VC* iii.23. **46** *VC* iii. 6. I differ from Charles-Edwards, 'Social background' 44, who takes Adomnán to refer here to the man's monastic *peregrinatio*; cf. ibid. 45–6, 53 n. 38. **47** *VC* iii. 22. **48** *VC* iii. 23.

'kings of the Irish', *Scotorum reges*, to those of 'foreign nations', *exterae gentes*, Adomnán echoes, no doubt consciously, the contrast drawn in his First Preface between the Irish language and the languages of the same (one assumes) *exterae gentes*.[49] The kings of the Irish included the king of Scottish Dál Riata; according to Adomnán, Columba had ordained Aedán as king (in 574) and identified and blessed his successor.[50] The story of Columba's passing, as retold by Ó Domhnaill in 1532, betrays again a focal shift. Here the saint foretells that not only will the 'kings of Scotland', *righthe na hAlban*, and its peoples honour Iona, but also other 'kings and peoples of the world', *righthe ⁊ cinedha an domain*, and 'the saints and patrons ... of Ireland and Scotland', *naeimh ⁊ patruin ... Erend ⁊ Alban*.[51] These terms carry the same implication as allusions, which I quoted at the outset, to Columba's 'separation from the Irish', *delughadh re Gaidhealaibh*, and to his 'exile', *deoraidhecht*, in 'foreign distant lands', *tírtha ciana comhaighecha*.[52] But in Adomnán's terms Columba never parted from the Irish, and Iona (with, presumably, its Dál Riata hinterland) is *excluded* from the definition of 'foreign distant lands'. Whether for rhetorical purposes or in response to a genuine parting of the ways, Ireland and Scotland are discontinuous in Ó Domhnaill's eyes. But for Adomnán in the seventh century, and probably for Columba in the sixth, Irish geography was a continuity of which Ireland was only one part.

ACKNOWLEDGMENTS

I am grateful to Thomas Clancy and Máire Herbert for their comments on a draft of this paper, although I alone am responsible for the views expressed.

---

49 Patrick refers to the *Irish* in *Epistola* § 10 as *gens extera*: Divine, *A computer-generated concordance*. **50** *VC* iii. 5, i. 9. **51** *BCC* § 361. Herbert points out that the late tenth-century *Saltair na Rann* lists the kings of Alba among native, as opposed to foreign, kings, indicating 'that the new kingship [of *Alba*] which united Pict and Gael, was now being given place in the conceptual scheme of Irish politics': 'Sea-divided Gaels, constructing relationships between Irish and Scots *c.*800–1169', in B. Smith (ed.) *Britain and Ireland 900–1300: Insular responses to medieval European change* (Cambridge, 1999), 87–97, at 90. Ó Domhnaill, by contrast, suggests the separation of *Éire* and *Alba*, culminating in the revelation (*BCC* §§ 371–4) that Columba's body had been brought by divine intervention to Downpatrick, Co. Down, to lie with those of Patrick and Brigid in fulfilment of their several prophecies. **52** *BCC* §§189, 190, 196, 378.

Representations of St Patrick

PETER HARBISON

In the context of a conference dedicated to the early history of Christianity in Fingal, held in a town which has an offshore island and a church dedicated to St Patrick, it was felt appropriate that the programme should include some contribution on the National Apostle himself. This took the form of a slide presentation with an appropriate commentary which is reproduced here in an altered and abbreviated form, together with a selection of the pictures used to illustrate the talk.

Probably the earliest-known *clearly identifiable* representation of St Patrick is scarcely much earlier than the year 1300, by which time he was dead for 800 years, but there are other earlier figures which *may* represent the Saint and help to fill the gap. Perhaps the earliest of these is high up on the north side of a cross nestling in the shadow of the Round Tower at Kells and bearing an inscription naming it as the 'Cross of Patrick and Columba'. Dating to around the ninth century, the cross bears a sculpture of two seated figures, one holding what may be a book or panel with a ringed cross on it (fig. 6.1). There is no parallel on the Irish High Crosses for these two figures, but they may well represent the two saints named in the inscription, and if that holding the Celtic cross were to be seen as St Columba (on whose island monastery of Iona there are also ringed high crosses), then the other figure could well be that of St Patrick.

We then have to move forward a further three centuries before coming to the next possible representations of the saint in the period between 1100 and 1200. One is the bishop-like figure back to back with the crucified Christ on a High Cross on St Patrick's Rock at Cashel in Co. Tipperary, which is traditionally identified as St Patrick (fig. 6. 2), but the identity of figures robed as bishops found on twelfth-century crosses has yet to be established beyond doubt. Not even tradition can be used to support the identification of another High Cross figure as St Patrick, yet its location could be seen to speak in favour of such a

6.1 Possible figures of Saints Patrick and Columba on a High Cross at Kells
(photo: P. Harbison)

6.2 A bishop (traditionally identified as St Patrick) on the twelfth-century
High Cross on the Rock of Cashel (photo: Dúchas)

hypothesis. This is on a small 'High Cross' now placed in the wall in the
cathedral at Downpatrick, Co. Down, near where the saint is thought to
have died (though we do not, in fact, know where he was buried). This
figure holds a staff or crozier and what is best taken to be a reliquary

6.3 Possible figure of St Patrick with reliquary on a cross in
Downpatrick cathedral (photo: P. Harbison)

6.4 St Patrick pierces foot of King Óengus of Cashel while baptizing him

with 'finials' on top (fig. 6.3). We know from Giraldus Cambrensis[1] that John de Courcy claimed around 1183 to have found relics of saints Patrick, Brigid and Columba at Downpatrick – a public relations coup needing a great leap of faith to believe – but, if the cross could be dated stylistically to around this period, it is quite possible that this could represent St Patrick holding a reliquary containing his relics. The smaller figure on the shorter cross adjacent to it could then possibly be interpreted as St Brigid.

Coming onto firmer ground, the earliest recognisable painting of St Patrick is in a French manuscript, HM 3027 in the Huntington Library

1 Gerald of Wales, *The history and typography of Ireland*, ed. J.J O'Meara (London, 1982), 105, 97.

6.5 St Patrick on the *Domhnach
Airgid* Shrine (photo: National
Museum of Ireland)

in California.[2] Dating from around 1300, it contains Jacopo de Voragine's *Legenda Aurea* (or 'Golden Readings') which, among other things, tells the tale of St Patrick accidentally putting the butt of his crozier through the foot of King Óengus of Cashel as he was baptizing him – an unfortunate slip which the monarch bore with fortitude because he thought it was part of the ceremony. This is precisely the scene illustrated in the manuscript (fig. 6.4), but the St Patrick represented here owes little to any earlier Irish pictorial tradition, and is depicted with beard and tonsure and, one suspects, very much in the guise of a medieval friar.

The beginnings of St Patrick being shown as a bishop go back to the middle of the fourteenth century – both inside and outside Ireland. In a fascinating fresco that came to light some twenty years ago in a convent in the Umbrian town of Todi,[3] the named figure of St Patrick stands on a hill, dressed in mitre and crozier, and putting his short staff (the *Bachall Iosa?*) into a hole beneath which are individual cavities naming the Seven Deadly Sins and containing suffering figures. Beside him is a nobleman, to whom he is obviously showing the horrors of Purgatory, though precisely how the tale of St Patrick's Purgatory managed to get to Todi has not yet been satisfactorily explained. At around the same time, but closer to home, the saint is shown clean-shaven, mitred and with epicopal cross-staff on the *Domhnach Airgid*,[4] now in the National

2 P. Harbison, 'The oldest legend', *Ireland of the Welcomes* (March-April 1979), 10–11.
3 N. MacTreinfhir, 'The Todi fresco and St Patrick's Purgatory, Lough Derg', *Clogher Record*, 12 (1986), 141–58.   4 M. de Paor, 'The relics of St Patrick', *Seanchas Ardmhaca*, 4 (1961),

6.6 St Patrick between St Dominic and St Francis above the north doorway of
the cathedral at Clonmacnois, Co. Offaly (photo: P. Harbison)

Museum (fig. 6.5). In the following century, he is shown on another
shrine – this time that of his own tooth.[5] The O'Dea crozier, of 1418,
now displayed in the Hunt Museum in Limerick,[6] may be the first time
that one of St Patrick's most famous attributes makes its appearance,
namely his trampling on the snake or snakes.

Returning to stonework, we find a smiling saint, with chasuble,
maniple and crozier flanked by SS. Francis and Dominic above the
north doorway of the cathedral at Clonmacnois, Co. Offaly (fig. 6.6).

87–91. The illustrations in various sections of this journal are the only serious effort to give an
overview of the changing iconography of St Patrick other than the article of Henry Morris,
'The iconography of St Patrick', *Journal of the Down and Connor Archaeological and Historical
Society*, 7 (1936), 5–29. **5** J. Raftery, *Christian art in ancient Ireland*, ii (Dublin, 1941), plate
119. **6** J. Hunt, *The Limerick Mitre and Crozier* (no date) 16, with plate xv.

6.7 Carving of St Patrick on
a stone from Faughart,
Co. Louth (photo: National
Museum of Ireland)

The portal was erected by Dean Odo – Aodh Ó Maoleoin – sometime around 1460, and I have suggested elsewhere[7] that it may have been intended to commemorate what readers of the old Irish Annals would have taken to be the millennium of the death of St Patrick in 461. The saint is found also as a 'weeper' decorating the sides of box tombs in the fifteenth and sixteenth centuries, though only on rare occasions are we enabled to identify any bishop figure as St Patrick either through inscription – as on the James Rice tomb in Waterford cathedral[8] – or through reptiles as on that of Bishop Wellesly, formerly in Great Connell and now in Kildare cathedral.[9] On the latter he is even distinguished with a *pallium*, the garment given to archbishops, and he also has reptiles beneath his feet. On these late medieval tombs, he is mostly clean-shaven. The reptiles again make their appearance on an attractive carving from Faughart in Co. Louth (fig. 6.7), now in the National Museum, where St Patrick is also clean-shaven, and has three crosses, one on top of the mitre, a second on the front of it, and a third on his breast. The snakes

7 P. Harbison, 'A St Patrick anniversary', *Ireland of the Welcomes* (March-April 1986), 13.
8 J. Hunt, *Irish medieval figure sculpture, 1200–1600* (Dublin/London, 1974), ii, plate 272.
9 Ibid., plate 220.

6.8 Figure of St Patrick at Patrickswell, Co. Limerick (photo: Michael Diggin)

also feature on a carving of uncertain date (fig. 6.8) above the well in the Limerick village of Patrickswell.

By the seventeenth century, the saint's beard becomes thick and long, to give him a respectable biblical appearance comparable to Moses, in an effort to boost his case for international recognition in the wake of the Council of Trent – the whole background to this development being cogently argued in a fascinating article by Bernadette Cunningham and Raymond Gillespie.[10] In Thomas Messingham's *Florilegium Insulae Sanctorum*, published in Paris in 1624, he is shown both on the title page

---

10 B. Cunningham and R. Gillespie, '"The most adaptable of the saints": the cult of St Patrick in the seventeenth century', *Archivium Hibernicum*, 49 (1995), 82–105.

6.9 St Patrick on the title page of Messingham's
Florilegium Insulae Sanctorum
(photo: Petra Schnabel)

(fig. 6.9) and on an internal illustration as robed in the baroque
vestments of a Tridentine bishop. This stereotype of the heavily bearded
bishop was to remain for centuries, Tiepolo even using it in a large

canvas of 1746 now in the Museum Civico in Padua.[11] Various other illustrations of the National Apostle from the eighteenth century have usefully been assembled in Bridget McCormack's well-researched *Perceptions of St Patrick in Eighteenth-Century Ireland* (Dublin, 2000).

The bearded bishop remained the archetypal representation of the saint throughout the nineteenth century, with sadly little variation among the myriad of St Patrick statues and stained-glass windows at the time. But towards the end of the Victorian era a certain expansion in patrician iconography emerges in the occasional use of narrative scenes, as found in the triple-light window at the western end of Kildare cathedral, where the saint is shown herding sheep in one panel and, in another, listening to the voice of the Irish in a dream. The contrast between stereotype and innovation is vividly experienced in the church at Kilcurry, a few miles north-west of Dundalk.[12] The choir has one window of the bearded patriarchal saint, but others nearby and in the north transept have richly decorative representations of unusual events of local importance in the saint's life executed by Catherine O'Brien and Sarah Purser during the first two decades of the twentieth century. Local pride within the diocese of Armagh is revealed in one of the Catherine O'Brien windows, representing an angel saying to St Patrick that he should go northwards to Armagh (fig. 6.10) 'for St Patrick loved the flowery fields of Louth'! O'Brien was also involved in painting the Purser windows featuring St Patrick and St Sechnell, and Patrick at the ford of Uililaigh (fig. 6.11), with the bearded saint dressed not as a bishop, but with a long tunic and cloak, which makes him look like an Apostle.

The same escape from the tradition of St Patrick as bishop is also seen in Margaret Clarke's painting of the saint, now in the Hugh Lane Municipal Gallery of Modern Art in Dublin.[13] Her husband Harry Clarke's work now brings us finally to Fingal, where some of the most beautiful representations of the saint and his entourage are found among Clarke's windows in Belcamp College, at Balgriffin.[14] Here we have large

---

11 C. Wheeler, 'Tiepolo's Patrick altarpiece', *Irish Arts Review*, 2, no. 1 (1985), 32–5. **12** N. Gordon Bowe, D. Caron and M. Wynne, *Gazetteer of Irish stained glass* (Dublin, 1988), 66. **13** Illustrated in de Paor (as in footnote 4). **14** C. Connellan, *Story of the Belcamp College Chapel windows* (Dublin, no date).

6.10 Kilcurry church, Co. Louth. Catherine O'Brien's stained glass window of 1914 with an angel telling St Patrick to go north to Armagh (photo: P. Harbison)

6.11 Kilcurry church, Co. Louth. Sarah Purser window
(partially painted by Catherine O'Brien) of 1909
with St Patrick in a local scene
(photo: P. Harbison)

figures of various Irish saints beneath which are small panels with narrative illustrations. One window has the large figure of St Patrick with shamrock – another favourite attribute that began to become quite common in the eighteenth century. He carries a crozier and wears what looks more like a hat than a mitre. Beneath, the saint receives two

6.13 (*opposite page*) Belcamp College, Co. Dublin. Harry Clarke panel of 1926 showing St Patrick presiding over the bier of Ireland's first consecrated virgins, Eithne and Fedelma (photo: P. Harbison)

6.12 Harry Clarke 1926 window in Belcamp College, Co. Dublin, showing full figure of St Patrick (with his disciple St Benen), and a panel below in which he receives two young people into the church (photo: P. Harbison)

gloriously art-nouveau young people (fig. 6.12). Another panel depicts the equally beautiful figures of Eithne and Fedelma, Ireland's first consecrated women, being laid to rest with an angel at one end of the bier, and St Patrick and his followers at the other (fig. 6.13).

At the northern end of Fingal, the choir of the Catholic church in Balbriggan has a large stained-glass window of St Patrick carrying the shrine of his bell. The most westerly window in the north wall of the nave, probably a product of the Harry Clarke studios, has the saint as a shepherd boy in one panel and lighting the Paschal Fire on the Hill of Tara in another (fig. 6.14). Coming finally to Skerries, we find the parish

6.14 Balbriggan Catholic Church. Harry Clarke Studios panel (1930s) of
St Patrick lighting the paschal fire (left) and as shepherd (right)
(photo: P. Harbison)

6.15 Nineteenth-century print of St Patrick above the shrine in
St Patrick's church, Skerries (photo: P. Harbison)

6.16 Albert Power's statue of St Patrick outside the church in Skerries
(photo: P. Harbison)

church containing a typical nineteenth-century print showing St Patrick
overcoming the serpents as he is dressed as a bishop holding his crozier,
and with a High Cross and what looks like the Rock of Cashel in the
background (fig. 6.15). Outside, beside the entrance portico, there is a
statue of St Patrick in the wall, carved by Albert Power around 1930 and,
showing the saint in his typical episcopal robes (fig. 6.16), above a bronze
plaque reflecting a story of what happened to his goat when he first
arrived in Ireland. It is a symbol of how strongly the saint is associated
with the town which has been honouring him through this millennium
conference.

Church Island: a description

MICHAEL RYAN, KEVIN MOONEY,
FRANK PRENDERGAST, BARRY MASTERSON

In truth Patrick came with Gauls to the islands of Moccu Chor (the Uí Chorra): to the eastern island known as Patrick's Island. With him there was a crowd of holy bishops, priests, deacons, exorcists, porters and lectors, as well as boys whom he ordained. Blessed by God, he came up from the sea at sunrise onto the Plain of Brega, with the true son of marvellous doctrine, bringing light to the darkness of ignorance …

Tírechán (later seventh century AD)

The seventh-century writer, Bishop Tírechán, wrote that Inishpatrick (known to locals invariably as Church Island)[1] off Skerries was the first place on which St Patrick set foot on his return to Ireland as a missionary. Skerries lies on the east coast – on the edge of the plain known anciently as Brega. It was on that plain, somewhere near the mouth of the Delvin river, that Patrick allegedly converted his successor Benignus, regarded as the first native Irishman to become a bishop. Legend has it that Benignus (Benén in Irish) received some of his education on Inishpatrick. On the island are the ruins of a twelfth- century church and associated buildings, probably living quarters for monks and a tomb-shrine. At one time there had also been a cemetery there.

Tírechán wrote his account of Patrick's arrival in the later seventh century. We cannot be sure that he was relying on a firm historical tradition, as he was very interested in recording legends of churches which had entered into some form of alliance with Armagh then pressing its claims to be the chief church of Ireland. Tírechán was interested in establishing the claims of Armagh to superiority over a wide network of religious houses. The great rival to Armagh was the family of churches

---

[1] Townland: Townparks; parish: Holmpatrick; barony: Balrothery East; OS 6", Co. Dublin, no. 5. The site is a registered monument SMR No. 005 019.

associated with St Columba (Colmcille) of Iona, which was represented in the area by a foundation at Lambay (it seems that Swords was established later).

The next historical reference to Church Island is the record in the annals of the raid on it by Vikings in AD 798, when the shrine of Do-Chonna (probably the stone tomb-shrine of the saint) was broken. It is often said that Lambay was the first place in Ireland to be attacked by Norsemen in 795, but this is probably an error as it shares its ancient name (*Rechru*) with Rathlin Island, which lay in the path of Vikings sailing from the Hebrides. It is inconceivable that three years would have passed before nearby Church Island was attacked. The island is exposed to powerful sea gales and was probably then, as now, bare of trees and any settlement on it would have been openly visible and defenceless.

References to the island after AD 798 are few.[2] If the monastery went into rapid decline after the Norse raids it enjoyed a revival – if not a refoundation – in the ninth century when it is recorded that Mael-Finnia mac Flannacáin, a member of the royal house of Brega died on the island as abbot in 903 and, in 1124, there is a further record of the death of the learned priest Máel-Cholaim on Inishpatrick. Both were prominent figures, which seems to indicate that the church on the island was significant at least within the region. That it was important is signalled by the fact that a generation or so later, in 1148, a synod was convened on the island by a number of bishops and St Malachy.[3] This assembly of over two hundred – priests and bishops – was summoned to nominate delegates to travel to Rome to obtain the *pallia* or insignia of archbishops signifying the re-integration of the Irish church with the Roman system of discipline and organization after centuries of diverging practices. The island was almost certainly chosen as the site of the synod for the symbolic reason that it was claimed by Tirechán as the first landfall of Patrick the missionary. It is very likely that the present church was built after the synod took place. Inishpatrick became a house of Augustinian monks before the Norman invasion of AD 1169, perhaps even by the time of the synod. In the early thirteenth century the

---

2 The early medieval history of the church is discussed in detail by MacShamhráin below.
3 A. Gwynn and R.N. Hadcock *Medieval religious houses in Ireland* (repr. Dublin 1988), 193; see discussion below by M. Holland.

monastery was moved to the mainland at the instance of Henry of London, archbishop of Dublin.[4] The site chosen was at Holmpatrick where the modern cemetery and Church of Ireland church now stand. Stones from the medieval monastery can be seen in the graveyard including the memorial of the last prior, Peter Mann. The name Holmpatrick combines the Scandinavian placename element *holm*, an islet, with the personal name Patrick. It is a variation of Inishpatrick.

THE ISLAND

The island (fig. 7.1), excluding rocks and beach, is 6.33 hectares (15.65 acres) in extent. It is about twice that when the rocks and beach are added. It is 465m long and 187m wide. It stands 14.5m above sea level at the highest point at the south-eastern corner. The eastern side of the island, especially towards the southern end drops steeply towards the sea, which has a fringe of reefs. The underlying rocks are of carboniferous limestone and shale, quite sharply folded – the bedding planes of the rock at the highest point are steeply canted being just a few degrees off the vertical. The stone may be prised off in fairly neat tabular slabs suitable for building, and the church, with the exception of tufa ornamentation, appears to be constructed of stone from the island. The normal landing point is Church Lane – a narrow entrance cut through the rocks on the western side of the island. Also on the west side, along the beach south of Church Lane is an artificial terrace created by a wall of crude, drystone masonry containing what was probably a garden. Its age is unknown. Overgrown with mallows, food remains – animal bone, mollusc, crab and lobster shells – are mixed in the soil. Whether the garden is ancient and associated with the church cannot be asserted without independent dating evidence.

The faint traces of a bank, probably ancient, run around the greater part of the island along the crest of the slope. It is visible on aerial photographs. Whether it is very ancient and associated with the ecclesiastical foundation or constructed later, partly to protect livestock

---

4 See note 3 above. Also N. Donnelly, *Short histories of Dublin parishes* pt. xvi, *Parishes of Lusk, Rush, Skerries and Balbriggan*, 87 repr. as Carraig Chapbooks (Blackrock, Co. Dublin, 1977).

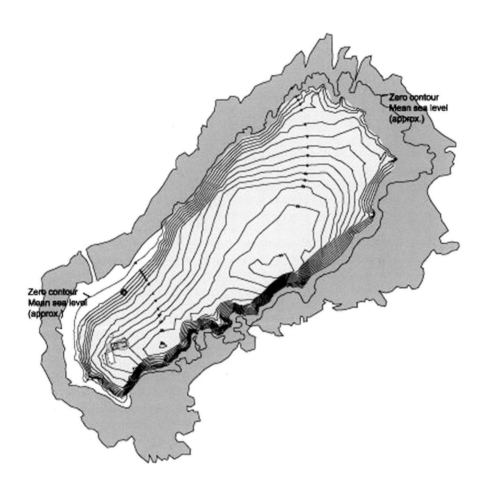

7.1 St Patrick's Island, Skerries, Co. Dublin
(Ryan, Mooney, Prendergast & Masterson)

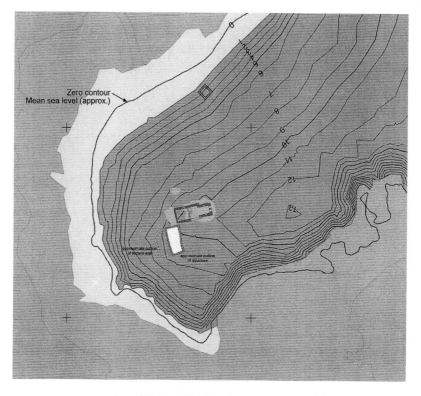

Zero contour.
Mean sea level (approx.)

approximate outline
of terrace wall

approximate outline
of structure

7.2 Site of St Patrick's Church, St Patrick's Island

is a moot point. The church buildings lie just below the highest point at the southern end of the island (fig. 7.2), partly sheltered from east winds by rising ground but exposed towards the other points of the compass. They were built on ground that had been artificially levelled by means of a terrace. Although inhabited in the nineteenth century by agricultural workers for at least part of the year, and once host to a substantial synod, the island has now no visible spring or other water source. It is likely that rainwater sumps exist but the dense growth of grass obscures many features.

THE CHURCH RUINS

The church is divided into two parts – a nave (the main part) for the congregation and a chancel where the altar was placed (fig. 7.6). The

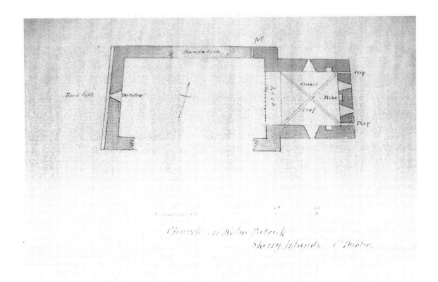

7.3 Du Noyer's plan of St Patrick's Church

7.4 Du Noyer watercolour; north window of chancel – exterior

East Windows. Old Church on Holm Patrick Skerry Islands. Cᵒ Dublin.

7.5 Du Noyer watercolour; east windows – interior

chancel had a stone roof supported on a groin vault. The nave was slated, or shingle-roofed. The nave is 14.3ms long (46.7 ft) and the chancel just over 6m (19.9 ft). The chancel vault appears to have collapsed some time in the eighteenth century, filling the area to a depth of over a metre with rubble. Its north wall is best preserved and there is evidence in its stonework that the usual arch separated the nave and chancel. There were two round-headed windows in the east wall of the chancel, one each in its north and south walls and one in the north wall of the nave. There is a small niche in the south wall of the chancel. A further niche between the two east windows recorded in Du Noyer's (1865) drawing (fig. 7.5) may be an error on the part of the artist as there is now no evidence for it (but see below). The east gable was pierced by a small window high up. The church door was probably on the south side, a feature of later twelfth-century buildings (fig. 7.6 – see also Du Noyer's plan, fig. 7.3). The stones of the north window arch and of the

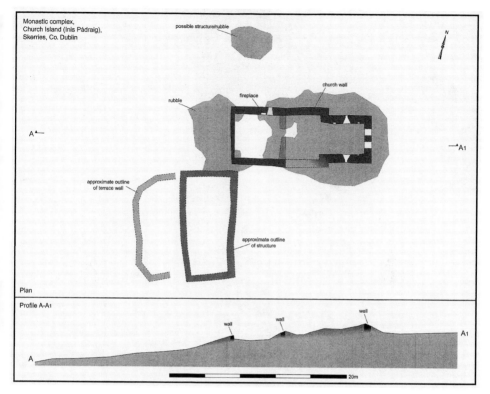

7.6 Plan of church site (Ryan, Mooney, Prendergast & Masterson)

roof were of calcareous tufa – an extremely light material, easy to shape (Du Noyer's watercolour, fig. 7.5, shows the interior of the east windows and fig. 7.4 shows the exterior of the north window of the chancel, with the tufa stones in place). Much of this was carried away in the last century for use in garden rockeries – and that, presumably, is when the east and south windows were robbed of their stones. One piece of tufa with a deep rebate cut in it was found during the survey of the church in 2000 at the nave-chancel junction. It probably formed part of the chancel arch. The stone is devoid of ornament and the chancel arch was probably therefore plain.

To the south of the church are the foundations of a narrow rectangular structure about 15 m in length, presumably a house for the monks (fig. 7.6 – prior to the survey carried out on the site, this feature had never been drawn). It is heavily overgrown and difficult to trace in places although it shows well in aerial photographs. It is clearly built on a terrace. On the north side of the church is a marked concentration of stones, sometimes interpreted locally as the site of a filled-in well or cistern. However, a more likely explanation is that it was some form of tomb-shrine, as suggested by Wakeman's early account (see below). Aerial photography hints that there may have been a sub-circular earthwork around the church originally but this may only be demonstrated by archaeological excavation.

The nave of the church was divided in two by a rough wall constructed to convert the west end into a shelter – presumably for herdsmen or agricultural labourers who must have worked for protracted periods on the island when it was tilled in the nineteenth century. It was equipped with a fireplace and chimney on the north wall. Mr Cochrane of Seapark had the island ploughed in the first half of the nineteenth century. It is reported that the workers found graves and a stone coffin. The coffin was brought to the mainland for use as a horse trough while Cochrane is said to have kept a skull from the island on the mantelpiece of his house.[5] A small house was built also in the nineteenth century, just above the beach on the western side. Animals were grazed on the island into the 1950s.

DESCRIPTIONS OF THE ISLAND

Isaac Butler's *Journal* of 1744 provides the first useful information on the physical state of the church, when he notes that its roof had lately fallen in.[6] There is no reason to disbelieve his account and we can conclude that the vault, at least, had stood until the first half of the eighteenth century.

The distinguished archaeologist, W.F. Wakeman, visited the island and its church sometime during his early career, and late in life provided

---

5 P.F. Moran in his edition of Mervyn Archdall's *Monasticon Hibernicum,* ii (Dublin 1876), 90, note 62 gives a somewhat sour account of this event: 'The remains of a very old church are still extant on the island, which, about fifty years ago was tilled by a Scotchman or Northern (sic) who settled in Skerries. The old cemetery was uprooted. And the tombstones etc. were thrown over the rocks into the sea: it is not unlikely that some ancient inscribed or sculptured memorials were irretrievably lost.' **6** *Isaac Butler's Journal 1744* Ms. Armagh Public Library (microfilm in National Library of Ireland) at p. 11 'Shipping; Holm Patrick next to it whereon

a note of it in the *Journal of the Royal Society of Antiquaries.* He describes the square-headed doorway as indicating the great age of the building.[7] However, there is something of a mystery here because there is no such door in the existing remains. In the *Dublin Saturday Magazine* the same author (initials erroneously given as W.W.F. instead of W.F.W.) had given an earlier account of the island in an article on Balrothery.[8] It is worth quoting in full (the emphasis is ours):

> The original establishment was in all probability upon Holmpatrick, or Inis Patrick, a small island lying at a short distance from the shore, nearly opposite the modern village. Upon this island St Patrick is said to have landed when on his voyage to the mouth of the Boyne. Tradition refers to the erection of a church *which still remains upon this island,* to the saint himself; and it is a very remarkable fact, whether the tradition be correct or not, that *the building referred to bears all the architectural characteristics of the oldest kind of sacred edifice erected in Ireland. The plan is a simple oblong of very small dimensions. Unfortunately the greater portion of the eastern gable, which no doubt carried a window, has fallen; the side walls are in moderately [ ] condition but contain no opening for the admission of light. In the centre of the western gable is a square-headed doorway so small that a full-sized man would have great difficulty in entering it. The sides have a considerable inclination from the ground upwards, and the walls which have a thickness unusual in buildings of the size of the church, appear to have been constructed without mortar.* We have examined in Kerry, Clare, Aran, and the other parts of Munster and Connaught, a number of early Christian edifices which have been declared on the authority of the late Drs. Petrie and O'Donovan to be as old at least as the 6th century and we have no hesitation in expressing our opinion that this little building, here for the first time noticed, must be regarded as belonging to the earliest period of Christianity in Ireland, and that in all probability it was erected under the immediate direction of St Patrick himself.

there is a large Abby now in Ruins, *the Roof lately fell in'* (emphasis added). **7** W.F. Wakeman, 'The ante-Norman churches of Dublin', *RSAI Jnl.,* 22 (1892), 104–5. **8** W.F. Wakeman, *Dublin Saturday Magazine,* ii, no. 58 (1876), 61–2.

> *Adjoining the earlier church, to the southward,* are the ruins of a daim-liag or great stone church, which bears evidence of having been erected in the earlier part of the 12th century. Its eastern window is formed of *acutely-pointed lancets,* and as was not uncommon in churches of the time, the whole of the chancel was closed in and roofed with stone. A very unusual circumstance in connexion with this church may be here recorded. The late Dr Petrie has stated to the writer that some thirty-five years or so ago, when examining the ruin, he picked from the mortar or grouting of the interior of the wall two small and very perfect arrow-heads formed of flint, and exactly similar to many specimens usually found in connexion with pagan and prehistoric interments. We have seen these singular relics, which differ in no respect from the arrowheads found so frequently in almost every part of Ireland, and which are generally designated 'elf-stones' by our country people who sometimes apply them to superstitious purposes. It is difficult to believe that weapons tipped with flint were used in the warfare of the British Islands so late as the period of the erection of the church. Could these 'elf-stones' have been introduced by the masons or builders as a 'charm'? [*sic*] This church is said to have been erected by Sitric Mac Murchad in the 9th century, but no portion of the present building is older than the 12th.

This description by Wakeman is of great importance. It clearly records a different structure, remarked upon by no one else, to the *north* of the church ruins. This was church-like in shape, apparently constructed of drystone masonry with a small lintelled doorway. Sadly he gave us no measurements but the description could indicate the former existence of a small tomb-shrine structure such as still exist at Banagher, Co. Derry and Clooney, Inishowen, Co. Donegal. St Keiran's church at Clonmacnoise, the traditional burial place of the saint, is a diminutive church, although clearly somewhat larger that that described on Church Island. It is likely that the concentration of stones north of the church and marked on the plan (fig. 7.6) as 'possible structure/rubble' is the site of structure described by Wakeman. It is quite distinct from the collapsed material from the church. It would repay archaeological investigation.

By the time G.V. Du Noyer planned the building in 1865 (figs. 7.3–5) and sketched the interior, the chancel area was filled almost up to the level of the windows with rubble from the collapsed vault. The state of the nave is unknown, but it is much less filled with rubble today. On Du Noyer's drawings[9] the windows retain their round-headed shaped tufa arches. Although he incorporates a third feature – a pointed niche – between the two windows of the east windows – there is no evidence that they were of the lancet form mentioned by Wakeman. Perhaps Wakeman's memory was playing tricks and there really had been a niche where Du Noyer indicated, but one entirely made of stucco of which no trace survives. He may then have confused in his memory the pointed shape of that niche with the very different round-headed windows. This is all very frustrating as Wakeman was a fine artist and recorder of ancient sites – his survey of the monastery of Inishmurray, Co. Sligo, is an exemplary work.

In 1888, Robert Walsh in his book *Fingal and its Churches* published two woodcuts of the church (figs. 7.7 and 7.8), which show much of the dressed stone already robbed from the windows in the east gable. The drawings also show some flagstones of the roof surviving on the north side. Today only a couple of stones are *in situ* to testify to the slope of the roof. The pictures are based on two watercolours (by NH: Nathaniel Hone) in the archives of the Representative Church Body. However, the view of the interior of the nave is peculiar in that the artist seems to have turned the north wall inside out in order to show the carved tufa of the widow and the springers of the groin-vaulting, a view which is impossible. Apart from that caveat, the views show the church pretty much as it is today. Walsh was unaware of the small structure which Wakeman had described and makes no mention of it.

A contemporary description by Dix in 1892 contains no mention of the small structure, which seems to have been demolished by then either by the work of tillage undertaken by Cochrane or by the depredations of

---

9 Royal Irish Academy Library Du Noyer, vii, 45–47 reproduced here by kind permission of the Academy.

7.7 North-east view – exterior (Walsh)

7.8 South-west view – interior (Walsh)

the cattle grazing on the island. Amongst the other information he describes the condition of the tufa (honeycombed by erosion), the fact that cattle occasionally shelter in the church and the presence of the conventual building to the south.[10] The description is also worth quoting in full:

> I visited in company with another member of our Society, the island of Skerries, called Inispatrick (St Patrick's Island), or Church Island, on which are the remains of the undoubtedly ancient church belonging to the monastery at one time on this island. It is quite exposed and unprotected, not only to storm and rough weather, but also to the cattle which graze on the island and appear to herd or be herded in the nave of the church, greatly to its disadvantage as well as profanation. The tufa stone at the wall angles, edge of roof and remains of groined arches in the chancel, has become honeycombed like a sponge, but still holds good. A simple post and wire paling, strongly made, to keep out the cattle, and some steps taken to cleanse the inside of the church, and to replace fallen stones in the walls would not cost much, and would help to preserve this ancient church. The debris inside to be cleared out, down to the original floor. The nave has evidently, in later days, been built up for a cattle shed, though now roofless. The island belongs to the Hamiltons of Balbriggan, but is by them let to a local farmer or grazier. Adjoining the church on the south or south-west, is the clearly-marked site of buildings no doubt belonging to the original monastery. The island is well worthy of a visit also from the geological point of view. Traces of lead ore appear in the quartz rock. There are no graves inside the church and it is not easy to identify any outside it.

A number of photographs of the church in the records of the Old Skerries Society – undated, although clearly of late nineteenth and early twentieth-century date – show that from the time of the Hone drawings, relatively little change has taken place in the condition of the church except what may be accounted for by gradual attrition by the elements.

10 E.M. Dix, *RSAI Jnl.*, 22 (1892), 180–1.

7.9 Church of St Patrick, St Patrick's Island;
north wall of chancel (M. Ryan)

The National Museum files contain photographs (undated but probably of the 1920s or 30s) by T.H. Mason, which record conditions not much different to today's. These show the north window almost intact as it is today, the east windows robbed of their tufa, and the interior full of collapsed masonry almost to the base of the east windows and extensive undergrowth within the chancel.

7.10 Church of St Patrick, St Patrick's Island; east windows (M. Ryan)

In 1966, the late Percy Le Clerc (fig. 7.9), Inspector of National Monuments, visited the site and drew an accurate sketch plan of the church. He noted that all the carved stone was of calcareous tufa and that the remaining masonry was of calp (limestone) quarried on the island. He noted the construction of what he called a cattle shed from the material of the nave. His opinion was that the church:

> … was a good example of French architecture of about 1100; but, allowing for a time-lag, it was probably built about 1130–1140. It is about the same date, or earlier, than the oldest parts of the abbey church of Mellifont (of which very little remains); it could be the first church to have been built in Ireland by French masons; it certainly is the best preserved early example of French building here and, so far as I know, it is the unique example of the style. It may of course have been built especially for the synod of 1143 (?) in

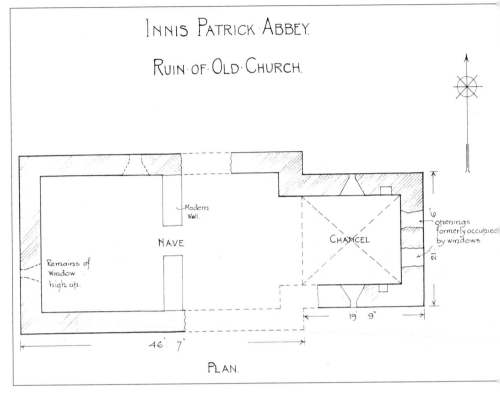

7.11 Sketch-plan of the church, 1966 (Le Clerc)

which case it would be almost exactly contemporary with the earliest parts of Mellifont; but, stylistically, it could be earlier than Cormac's Chapel at Cashel (1134) … the church is exceptionally interesting in the history of the twelfth century Reformation and justifies exceptional measures for its preservation.[11]

Mr Le Clerc's remarks about the date of the church would find general support amongst architectural historians. Without independent dating evidence, when in the twelfth century it was built is open to debate. A brief summary of the course of early medieval Irish church architecture may be helpful. In the first phase of their development in the ninth and

11 File Office of Public Works. Report signed 'P. Le Clerc 1/9/66'.

tenth centuries, Irish stone churches were essentially simple unicameral rectangular structures with single, western, (usually) trabeate (that is lintelled) doorways of which we know little more.[12] They were often poorly lit by simple, sometimes single, windows and must therefore have been illuminated with lamps or candles. There is no surviving evidence that they were plastered and painted but it is possible that some of them were.[13] We have no evidence of original altars. There is likewise no evidence of internal arrangements, and no features such as ambo/pulpit, font, or fixtures for chancel rails survive. In the twelfth century there is a tendency for chancels to be added to unicellular churches, or built en suite with naves,[14] and southern doorways begin to make their appearance. At the cathedral of Kilmacduagh, for example, an older trabeate west door was blocked up and a southern entrance was created. The appearance of southern doorways may signal some liturgical change. The church on Inishpatrick/Church Island combined native tradition (the stone roof of the chancel) with fashionable new elements (the paired east windows, the en suite chancel, the groin vault and south doorway) when it was built, perhaps as a result of Augustinian influence. This may well as Le Clerc believed, have been a result of French influence, a natural consequence of the affiliations of the order. Whether the church was already standing at the time of the synod or whether it was built in commemoration of it is an open question.

SUMMARY AND CONCLUSIONS

The ecclesiastical settlement on Church Island, in its latest phase, consisted of a nave-and-chancel church built in the twelfth century, a conventual building, presumably quarters for the community, to the south of it and possibly a small tomb shrine in the form of a miniature church to the north. The presence of an earthwork around the church site is worthy of some further investigation as is the nature of the terrace

---

12 The classic study is Harold Leask, *Irish churches and monastic buildings, i: the first phases and the Romanesque period* (Dundalk, 1955). **13** Maurice Craig, *The architecture of Ireland from the earliest times to 1880* (London and Dublin, 1989), 31. **14** Craig, *The architecture of Ireland*, 39–40; Tadhg O'Keefe, 'Architectural traditions of the early medieval church in Munster', in Michael A. Monk and John Sheahan (eds) *Early medieval Munster*, (Cork, 1998), 112–24 at 121.

feature on the shoreline, which may have been a garden for the settlement. Nineteenth-century agricultural activity on the site unearthed a number of graves and their markers were, it is said, thrown into the sea. Without carrying them across jagged rocks, this would have been impossible and so there is a chance that some of these may lie on the beach near the site but the writers have not found any. The early history of the site, as analysed below by the editor, holds out the possibility that three phases of church development may be represented on the island – an early foundation phase, a tenth-century period of revival followed by a final phase culminating in the building of the present church. These may be archaeologically detectable.

The church is in need of some conservation and consolidation work. It may also be wise to clear the debris from inside the structure. Wakeman's description of a smaller structure north of the church should be tested by excavation.

Thanks are due to Skerries Lifeboat, Paddy and Conor McNally, Inez Hagen, Roger Stalley, Tom Condit, Peter Harbison, Victor Reijis, Fr. Leo Quinlan and above all, Maree Baker for many references and even more patience. The Royal Irish Academy generously permitted the reproduction of the Du Noyer drawings in their Library and thanks are due to Petra Schnabel and the Librarian Siobhán Fitzpatrick for their kindness.

Church and dynasty in Early Christian Brega: Lusk, Inis Pátraic and the case of Máel-Finnia, king and saint

AILBHE MAC SHAMHRÁIN

Kings as heads of churches are well attested in the early Irish historical record,[1] however strange this may seem from a modern perspective. The fact that most kings were married men (some, indeed, much married – although there were a few religious celibates), and were not necessarily in holy orders, presented no obstacle to holding senior office in the Irish church, at least until the twelfth-century ecclesiastical reform.[2] For much of the Early Christian period, celibacy was not compulsory for Irish clergy; nor was it a requirement that heads of churches – whether or not they were royal persons – be priests. This was the era of the so-called 'lay abbots' – in fact a rather exclusive group whose members belonged to the upper echelons of society, and who were presumably in some clerical grade, even minor orders. The system, then, facilitated those who sought to combine dynastic and religious functions, in spite of the worldliness generally associated with royals. However, for a king to be acknowledged as a saint was another matter.

In other societies, including Anglo-Saxon England and medieval Scandinavia, kings were sometimes proclaimed saints not because they held any church office, but because their policies (or actions) were deemed to have advanced the Christian cause.[3] However, those

---

1 Especially in *Leth Moga* (the southern half of Ireland); for example Muiredach (d. 885; *AU*) son of Bran, king of the Leinstermen was *princeps* (superior) of Kildare; several Munster overkings held ecclesiastical office; Ólchobur (d. 797; *Ann. Inisf.*), son of Flann of Uí Fidgeinti, was *abb* (abbot) of Inis Cathaig; Éoganachta king Fedelmid son of Crimthann entered into *abbthaine Corcaige* ('the abbacy of Cork') in 836 and occupied *suide abbad* (the abbatial seat) of Clonfert in 840 (*Ann. Inisf.*), while Cormac (d. 908) son of Cuilennán, who took the kingship of Cashel in 901 (*Ann. Inisf.*), is described as in *t-uasalepscop & in macc óg* ('the noble bishop and celibate'). 2 For a discussion of authority within the pre-reform Irish Church, see Colmán Etchingham, *Church organisation in Ireland, AD 650 to 1000* (Maynooth, 1999), 47–104. 3 For example, Oswald

commemorated as saints in the Irish tradition (pre twelfth-century reform) have not been canonised – but owed their saintly status to the fact that they founded churches, and because it was believed that they had miraculous powers as proof of sanctity. Therefore, the inclusion among the Irish saints (he is accorded a feast-day in the later martyrologies and features in Colgan's *Acta Sanctorum*; see below) of Máel-Finnia king of Brega, who does not belong to the age of the church founders and miracle-workers, but who does appear to have held church office at Inis Pátraic (St. Patrick's Island), while not unique,[4] calls for some investigation.

Máel-Finnia belonged to Síl nÁeda Sláine, a dynasty of the southern Uí Néill; specifically, he belonged to the lineage of Uí Chonaing (table 8.1) associated with Cnogba (Knowth, Co. Meath), descended from Conaing son of Congal who had been killed in an internal dynastic conflict in 662.[5] Síl nÁeda Sláine had been excluded from the kingship of Tara (the paramount kingship of Uí Néill) since the early eighth century; the last representative of the dynasty to have held that particular dignity was Cináed (sl. 728) son of Írgalach.[6] Later, Máel-Finnia's lineage managed to expropriate the kingship of Ciannachta Breg, a coastal territory which extended from the river Dee to the Delvin, at the expense of a local dynasty. The more successful Uí Chonaing rulers were styled kings of Cnogba, or kings of Brega, a region which encompassed southern Louth, most of Co. Meath and northern Co. Dublin. By the later ninth century, Uí Chonaing, having contracted judicious marriage-alliances – notably with Cenél nÉogain, a powerful dynasty of the northern Uí Néill which produced several kings of Tara – already aspired to a higher political destiny.

(d. 642) king of Northumbria; described by Bede, *Historia Ecclesia*, iii, §§1–3, 6, 9, 11–13; or the Norwegian king Ólafr Haraldsson (d. 1030), described by Adam of Bremen, *History of the archbishops of Hamburg-Bremen*, trans. F.J. Tschan (New York, 1975), 96–7; see Ailbhe MacShamhráin, *The Vikings: an illustrated history* (Dublin, 2002), 100, 102, 104.   **4** Note that Fedelmid (d. 847) son of Crimthann, king of Cashel, is included in the genealogies of the saints and in the martyrologies; LL 352f 30: *Book of Leinster*, ed. Anne O'Sullivan (Dublin, 1983), 1575; Pádraig Ó Riain (ed.), *Corpus Genealogiarum Sanctorum Hiberniae* (Dublin, 1985), 50; *Martyrology of Donegal*, ed. J. O'Donovan, J.H. Todd & W. Reeves (Dublin, 1864), at 28 August.   **5** Francis John Byrne, 'Historical note on Cnogba (Knowth)', *RIA Proc.*, 66 C (1968), 383–400.   **6** For Írgalach and Cináed see Ailbhe MacShamhráin & Paul Byrne, 'A prosopography of the personages named in the poems Baile Chuind and Arsiasar coimhdhi Temrae', 1: 28a, 32 in Edel Bhreathnach (ed.), *Tara kingship and landscape* (forthcoming).

Table 8.1 Lineages of Síl nÁedo Sláine

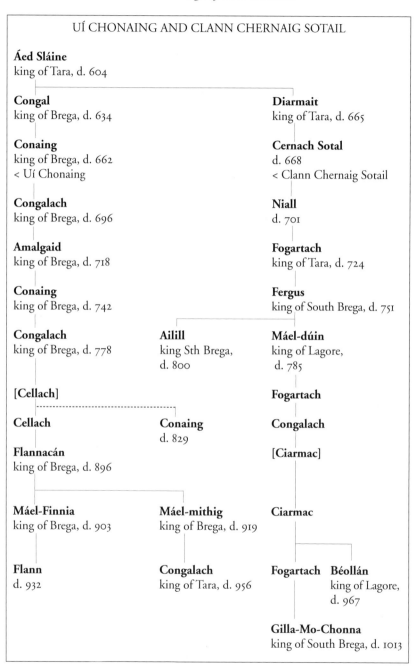

UÍ CHONAING AND CLANN CHERNAIG SOTAIL

Áed Sláine
king of Tara, d. 604

Congal
king of Brega, d. 634

Diarmait
king of Tara, d. 665

Conaing
king of Brega, d. 662
< Uí Chonaing

Cernach Sotal
d. 668
< Clann Chernaig Sotail

Congalach
king of Brega, d. 696

Niall
d. 701

Amalgaid
king of Brega, d. 718

Fogartach
king of Tara, d. 724

Conaing
king of Brega, d. 742

Fergus
king of South Brega, d. 751

Congalach
king of Brega, d. 778

Ailill
king Sth Brega,
d. 800

Máel-dúin
king of Lagore,
d. 785

[Cellach]

Fogartach

Cellach

Conaing
d. 829

Congalach

Flannacán
king of Brega, d. 896

[Ciarmac]

Máel-Finnia
king of Brega, d. 903

Máel-mithig
king of Brega, d. 919

Ciarmac

Flann
d. 932

Congalach
king of Tara, d. 956

Fogartach   **Béollán**
king of Lagore,
d. 967

Gilla-Mo-Chonna
king of South Brega, d. 1013

Máel-Finnia's father was Flannacán son of Cellach (table 8.2) who, in 868, succeeded Flann son of Conaing (a first cousin once-removed) in the kingship of Brega. His mother was Der-bhFáil (named in a verse accompanying his obit), daughter of Máel-dúin (d. 867) and a grand-daughter of the Cenél nÉogain king of Tara Áed Oirdnide (d. 819).[7] His own personal name means 'devotee of St Finnian', which suggests some family connection with the latter's foundation of Clonard (Co. Meath), more often associated with the Clann Cholmáin dynasty of the southern Uí Néill. It is possible that the *princeps* (superior) and *scriba optimus* (excellent scribe) of Clonard, Ferdomnach son of Flannacán, who died in 932, was his brother.[8] Certainly, Máel-Finnia had one full brother, Cellach *rígdamna Breg* ('one who was eligible for the kingship of Brega').[9] Apparently, he also had at least four half-brothers, including Donn-cuan, Congalach, Cináed (the latter two styled *rígdamna Breg* in the annals)[10] and the more illustrious Máel-mithig (d. 919) later king of Brega, whose mother was Eithne, a daughter of king of Tara Áed Finnliath (d. 879) and a first cousin once-removed of Der-bhFáil, continuing the dynastic connection with Cenél nÉogain.[11] There is no mention of Máel-Finnia's wife, but he had a son Flann (d. 932) and a daughter Der-bhFáil (d. 931).

Flannacán and his sons inherited a troubled kingship at the expense of a parallel Uí Chonaing line, headed by the sons of his cousin Conaing (d. 849). The Meath area, a patchwork of petty local kingships upon which the Uí Néill dynasties had imposed a sometimes uneasy overlordship, had long suffered from political unrest – even before the arrival of the Vikings. The district as a whole was subjected to Viking raids from an early stage; whatever the argument for identifying Rechru, plundered in 795, with Lambay as opposed to Rathlin, there is probably a better case for identifying Inis Pátraic – raided in 798, on which occasion the shrine of Do Chonna was broken – with Church Island.[12]

---

7 *AU* 903 names Der-bhFáil in a verse accompanying the obit of Máel-Finnia; Margaret C. Dobbs, 'The Ban-Shenchus, *Revue Celtique*, 47–9 (1930–2), 187. **8** *AU* 932; Paul Byrne, 'The community of Clonard, sixth to twelfth centuries', *Peritia*, 4 (1985), 165, 172, does not make this connection. **9** Dobbs, 'The Ban-Shenchus', 187. **10** These three are described as sons of Flannacán in their obits (*AU* 873, 893, 896); see Bart Jaski, 'Additional notes to the Annals of Ulster', *Ériu*, 48 (1997), 126, 127. **11** Dobbs, 'The Ban-Shenchus', 187; Rawlinson B 502, 144a 49; M.A. O'Brien (ed.), *Corpus Geneaogiarum Hiberniae* (Dublin, 1962), 160. **12** *AU* 795; the

Table 8.2 The family of Máel-Finnia

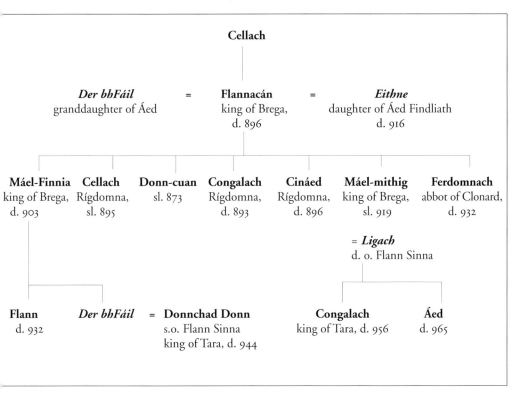

exact sequence is difficult to reconstruct; record at 794 of 'the spoiling of the sea islands between Ireland and Scotland'; is followed by an attack on Rechru at 795. Richard Sharpe, introduction to Adomnán of Iona, *Life of St Columba* (London, 1995), 82, identifies the island with Lambay, but identification with Rathlin is more widely accepted in recent literature; see Seán Duffy, *Atlas of Irish history* (Dublin, 1997), 25; C.D. Morris, 'Raiders, traders and settlers: the Early Viking Age in Scotland', in H.B. Clarke, M. Ní Mhaonaigh & R. Ó Floinn (eds), *Ireland and Scandinavia in the Early Viking Age* (Dublin, 1998), 73; J. Graham-Campbell, 'The Early Viking Age in the Irish Sea area' in ibid., 104; D. Ó Corráin, 'Viking Ireland – afterthoughts', in ibid., 436; *AU* 798 records the breaking of the shrine of Do Chonna, which Sharpe (1995, 82) suggested may have been that at Connor; however, the shrine is expressly associated with Inis Pátraic; in the nineteenth century, Todd had suggested St Patrick's Island off the Isle of Man, with which Do Chonna was also associated, but on balance, the notice probably does refer to the Skerries island (Ó Corráin 1998, 436); see above discussion by Dr M. Ryan et al.

Certainly, Lusk was plundered and burned by Vikings in 827 and, following the establishment of a permanent base at Dublin in 841 and the arrival of the Scandinavian magnate Ólafr the White in 853, there was increased pressure on the district as a whole with Lusk again burned in 856.[13] The then leaders of Uí Chonaing had been quick to form alliances with Viking bands, in their efforts to break the hegemony of the Clann Cholmáin and Cenél nÉogain dynasties. In 850, Cináed son of Conaing rebelled against his overlords and, with Viking support, wreaked havoc throughout Meath, attacking the crannóg of Lagore and the ecclesiastical site of Trevet before being captured and drowned by Máel-Sechnaill son of Máel-Ruanaid, king of Tara. His brother and successor, Flann son of Conaing, led a coalition, which included Leinster and Viking forces, against the next king of Tara, Áed Finnliath, but was defeated and killed at the battle of Cell ua nDaigri (perhaps Killineer townland, near Drogheda) in 868. Among the fallen on the winning side was Fachtna son of Máel-dúin, a brother of the above-discussed Der-bhFáil. It is possible that the alliance formed with Cenél nÉogain, whereby Flannacán married Der-bhFáil (a cousin of Áed Finnliath, later the mother of Máel-Finnia and Cellach), if it had not been entered into earlier, was an outcome of this battle and of a perceived need to rebuild relationships with one of the strongest Uí Néill dynasties.

Although the evidence is slight, it seems reasonable to assume that Flannacán was actively involved in building dynastic relationships with the church. The nature of his family connection with Clonard (mentioned above) is unclear, as is its time of origin. Presumably, it pre-dates the birth of his son Máel-Finnia, whose name reflects devotion to the founder-saint Finnian. A brief tenure of the headship of Clonard by Cormac (d. 885), bishop of Duleek, especially if it can be seen as a reflection of improved relationships with Clann Cholmáin, may be significant in this regard. Duleek, the foundation of which was ascribed to St Cianán, was situated in the Uí Chonaing heartland of northern Brega and was probably the most prestigious ecclesiastical site in the region. Here, however, the indications are that the principal church offices were held by the Ciannachta Breg, a local dynasty which had

---

13 *AU* 827, 841, 853, 856.

been politically suppressed by Síl nÁeda Sláine. The ruling lineage of these Ciannachta, although traced to an eponym Tadc mac Céin, and claiming a (probably fictitious) relationship with other local petty dynasties (including the Saithne of north Dublin and the Gailenga and Luigne of northern Meath),[14] was probably an artificially created amalgam of local lineages. Indeed, it has recently been suggested that their origins may be sought among the ecclesiastical tenantry of Duleek.[15]

Although reduced in political terms as vassals of Síl nÁeda Sláine, some of the more important lines of the Ciannachta Breg directed their energies into ecclesiastical affairs – becoming closely involved with several foundations south of the Delvin, in the territory of Saithne, which would later be drawn into the Hiberno-Scandinavian realm which the Irish called Fine Gall, or Fingal. Certainly, there are hints of a Ciannachta connection with Lambay. As has recently been shown, this is almost certainly the Columban Rechru, the foundation of which can be dated to 635 in the abbacy of Segéne; a Middle Irish poem, found in the manuscript Laud 615, relates an anachronistic foundation story in which St Columba (d. 597), with guarantees from kings of Uí Néill and Ciannachta, parcels out the land for his new church in the presence of St Mac-Cuilinn (d. 496).[16] Presumably, the intended reference is to the successors of these founder-saints. Of importance here is the mention of Mac-Cuilinn, commemorated as the founder and patron of Lusk, a site which has clear Ciannachta links. This local saint, who features in the Old Irish list of bishops, and who seems to have been broadly contemporary with St Patrick,[17] is fitted into Irish hagiography[18] and is provided with an Irish pedigree, his father named as Cathmogh and his mother as Fedelm, and traced – somewhat unconvincingly – to the

---

14 Francis John Byrne, *Irish kings and high kings*, new ed. (Dublin, 2001), 68–9. 15 Paul Byrne, 'Ciannachta Breg before Síl nÁeda Sláine', in A.P. Smyth (ed.), *Seanchas: studies in early and medieval Irish archaeology, history and literature in honour of Francis J. Byrne* (Dublin, 2000), 121–6. 16 Michael Byrnes, 'The Ard-Ciannachta in Adomnán's *Vita Columbae*', in Smyth (ed.), *Seanchas*, esp. 132. 17 De Episcopis, LL 365d 22; *Bk. Leinster*, vi, ed. A. O'Sullivan, 1649; *AU* 496 'Quies M.Cuilinn episcopi Luscan'; his feast-day is commemorated at 6 September; see *Martyrology of Tallaght*, ed. R.I. Best & H.J. Jackson (London, 1931); *Félire Óengusso*, ed. W. Stokes (London, 1905); *Mart. Donegal*. 18 *Fél. Óeng.*, note at 9 September, where Mac-Cuilinn informs Ciarán that the saints of Ireland had fasted against him so that he would have a short life on this earth.

Ciannachta.[19] Significantly, the medieval genealogists remark that Mac-Cuilinn was originally named Cuinnid, which seems British; certainly, one of his successors at Lusk, the bishop Petrán (d. 616), bore a British name.[20] It is therefore possible that Lusk was a British foundation, like certain neighbouring sites such as Lann Bechaire (Bremore, near Balbriggan), associated with, Saints Mo-Locé and Mo-Domnóc who (although provided with Irish pedigrees) are represented as pupils of St David of Menevia and may well have been British.[21]

Table 8.3 Ecclesiastical heads of Lusk

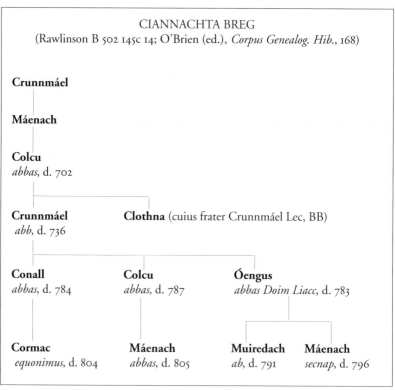

CIANNACHTA BREG
(Rawlinson B 502 145c 14; O'Brien (ed.), *Corpus Genealog. Hib.*, 168)

Crunnmáel

Máenach

Colcu
abbas, d. 702

Crunnmáel   **Clothna** (cuius frater Crunnmáel Lec, BB)
abb, d. 736

Conall   **Colcu**   **Óengus**
abbas, d. 784   *abbas*, d. 787   *abbas Doim Liacc*, d. 783

Cormac   **Máenach**   **Muiredach**   **Máenach**
equonimus, d. 804 *abbas*, d. 805   *ab*, d. 791   *secnap*, d. 796

19 LL 352g 54, 372b 33; *Bk. Leinster*, vi, 1576, 1694; Ó Riain, *Corpus Geneal. SS Hib.*, 52, 175; his father's alleged ancestor, Finchad (or Finchán) son of Fiacc, is usually associated with the Ciannachta of Glenn Gaimen (Dungiven, Co. Derry); see Rawlinson B 502, 128a 44, 145c 50, 153b 53; O'Brien, *Corpus Geneal. Hib.*, 98, 169, 246. **20** LL 352g 54, 354e 74; *Bk. Leinster*, vi, 1576, 1595; *AU* 616 'Mors Petrain episcopi Luscan'. **21** Mo Locé or Lochén son of Dub Dligid (20 January, *Mart. Tallaght, Fél. Óeng., Mart. Donegal*) is traced to Buán son of Mug

In any event, Lusk developed as an episcopal see, the large dimensions of its enclosure, and later the construction of a round tower at the site, attesting to its ecclesiastical (and, presumably, commercial) importance.[22] Lusk is a very well documented site, and the hereditary character of its abbacy has long been recognized.[23] Of more particular note is the fact that the leading ecclesiastics here, at least from seventh century and continuing into the ninth, belong to the Ciannachta Breg (see table 8.3) – hence, presumably, the pedigree assigned to Mac-Cuilinn. Already by the late eighth century, however, their Síl nÁedo Sláine overlords, especially Clann Chernaig Sotail the Lagore-based rulers of Southern Brega, were apparently making their presence felt at the site. On the feast of St Mac-Cuilinn, 6 September 800, Ailill son of Fergus, king of Southern Brega, died when thrown from his horse on the green of Lusk.[24] Before the middle of the ninth century, there is a break in the sequence of Ciannachta abbots, and a new group of hereditary church-men appear in the record – the family of one Ruaidrí and of his son Óenacán (see table 8.4). It so happens that the rare personal name of Óenacán occurs (in the published genealogies) only among a Síl nÁeda Sláine segment known as Clann Áeda Laigen, settled on the Leinster marchlands, and among the northern Leinstermen. The name Ruaidrí, although more widespread, is not in the Síl nÁeda Sláine genealogies but is found among their northern Leinster neighbours. It may be significant

Roth, which suggests an origin among the Fer Maige Féne (Fermoy, Co. Cork; see LL 351a 6; *Bk. Leinster*, vi, 1560); Mo-Domnóc or Dominicus, otherwise associated with Tipra Fachtnai (Tibberaghny, Co. Kilkenny; 13 February *Mart. Donegal*), is linked with Lann Bechaire by seventeenth-century scholar John Colgan, *Acta Sanctorum Hiberniae* (Louvain, 1645; repr. Dublin, 1947), 326–8, and is credited with the introduction of domestic bees to Ireland. However, the links with St David, and the placename element *Lann*, suggest British connections. For discussion of the Bremore site, see A. Gwynn & R.N. Hadcock, *Medieval religious houses: Ireland*, new ed. (Dublin & London, 1988), 396. **22** Leo Swan, 'Enclosed ecclesiastical sites', in T. Reeves-Smith & F. Hammond (eds), *Landscape archaeology in Ireland* (Oxford, 1983), 269 & plate 3; Brian Lalor, *The Irish Round Tower* (Cork, 1999), esp. 137–9. **23** Kathleen Hughes, *The church in Early Irish society* (London, 1966), 162, 211; the annal-record for Lusk up to the eleventh century includes twelve ecclesiastical heads (variously styled abbot, or *aircinnech* – superior), three vice-abbots, eleven bishops, four scribes, one lector and one steward. **24** *AU* 800 Ailill m. Fergusa rex deiscirt Bregh traiectus est de equo suo in circio ferie filii Cuilinn Luscan & continuo mortuus est; Rawl B 502, 144b 31; O'Brien, *Corpus Geneal. Hib.*, 160; Charles Doherty, 'Exchange and trade in Early Medieval Ireland', *RSAI Jnl.*, 110 (1980), 81, argues that the term *circius*, especially in the context of the Saint's feastday, indicates an *óenach*, or fair, at Lusk.

that one of Óenacán's sons, Tuathal (d. 929), held episcopal office at Duleek and Lusk, as well as being *maer* of the Patrician churches in Brega.[25] Admittedly, these considerations do not prove that the churchmen in question belonged to any Síl nÁeda Sláine lineage; however, in view of this apparent shift in the abbatial succession, the possibility that an ecclesiastical line acceptable to that dynasty had been installed at Lusk, before the advent to power of Flannacán and Máel-Finnia, deserves to be considered.

Table 8.4 Ecclesiastical heads of Lusk

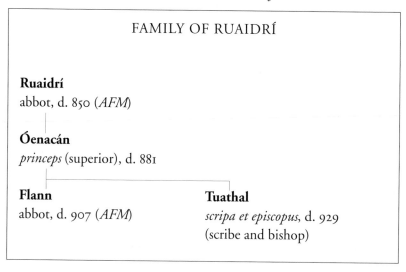

FAMILY OF RUAIDRÍ

Ruaidrí
abbot, d. 850 (*AFM*)

Óenacán
princeps (superior), d. 881

Flann
abbot, d. 907 (*AFM*)

Tuathal
scripa et episcopus, d. 929
(scribe and bishop)

From his accession to kingship in 868, Flannacán and his family had to contend with political conflict inside Síl nÁeda Sláine, in addition to external threats. There was opposition from their own cousins within Uí Chonaing, and from the rival lineage of Clann Chernaig Sotail, based around Lagore, which had declined in importance (its rulers were generally styled kings of *Deiscert Breg*, or Southern Brega – the area of north Co. Dublin). There were also difficulties with their neighbours to

---

25 *AU* 929; Etchingham, *Church organisation*, 183, 184, considers the case of Tuathal – and argues that the role of *maer* had legal and revenue gathering functions.

the north, the rulers of Conaille (northern Co. Louth), and – it seems – periodic hostilities with the Dublin-based Vikings. In 873, Donn-Cuan son of Flannacán was killed, in circumstances savouring of treachery, by Conaing son of Flann, his second-cousin once-removed. Whether the latter's capture and beheading by the Leinstermen in 884 owed anything to Flannacán is not stated. The prominent ecclesiastical site of Duleek, was attacked by Vikings in 881 and many prisoners taken; Barith, leader of the raiding-party, it is said, died at the hands of St Cianán – presumably a euphemism for a revenge-killing by the Duleek community. In 891, Cellach son of Flannacán had the king of Conaille beheaded, which seems to represent an act of vengeance although the preceding circumstances are not related. Four years later, Cellach was himself killed, also in treacherous circumstances ('dolose iugulatus est') by Fogartach son of Tolarc, a dynast of Clann Chernaig Sotail.[26] Of the other sons of Flannacán, two met a natural, if premature, death; Congalach in 893 and Cináed in 896.[27] That same year, Flannacán himself, aged presumably over seventy, was killed in a skirmish with the Norsemen of Dublin.[28]

Máel-Finnia, on succeeding his father, inherited a kingship which apparently had the capacity to exercise power at regional level. His relatively short reign (896–903) is marked by at least two quite impressive military achievements. In 897, he repelled an invasion from Ulaid (eastern Ulster), defeating the dynasties of Dál nAraide and Uí Echach Cobo at the battle of Ráith Cró (near Slane). The casualties included Mac-Étig, king of Dál nAraide (or his son Muiredach – the record is unclear), while the Uí Echach overking of Ulaid, Aidíth son of Láigne, who fled the field, was killed by his own retainers.[29] Ready and willing to capitalize on protracted dissensions within the Norse kingship of Dublin,[30] Máel-Finnia formed an alliance with Cerball son of

---

26 *AU* 895; Cellach mac Flannacáin, *rí[g]damna* Bregh nuile (one eligible for the kingship of all Brega), o Fhogartach mac Tolairg dolose iugulatus est. **27** *AU* 893, 896; Congalach … 'in pace quievit' (rested peacefully); Cellach … moritur (died); both men predeceased their father, while at least one half-brother, the above-mentioned Ferdomnach, lived on until 932. **28** *AU* 896 Flannacán mac Cellaig rí Breg a Nordmannis iugulatus est. While his father's obit is not recorded, the early ninth century obits of several uncles, and record of his brother Conaing's death in 829, would suggest that he was a septuagenarian at the time of his own death. **29** *AU* 897, 898; LL 41c 60, 41e 38–41; *The Book of Leinster,* i, ed. R.I. Best, O. Bergin & M.A. O'Brien (Dublin, 1954), 194, 195. **30** For discussion of conflict within the Dublin-Norse

Muireccán, the Uí Fáeláin overking of Leinster. In 902, they inflicted a severe defeat on the Norsemen and attacked their Dublin base with such force that the annalist declares:

> Indarba ngennti a hÉre i. longport Átha Cliath o Máel-Findia m. Flandacáin co feraibh Bregh & o Cerball m. Muiricáin co Laignibh; co farcabsat drecht mar dia longaibh co n-erlasat lethmarba iarna nguin & a mbrisiuth.
>
> (The expulsion of the heathens from Ireland i.e. from the fortress of Dublin by Máel-Finnia son of Flannacán with the men of Brega and by Cerball son of Muireccán with the Leinstermen; and they abandoned a good number of their ships and escaped half dead after they had been wounded and broken).[31]

This 'expulsion of the heathens' by Máel-Finnia and his allies should probably not be taken to mean that every Scandinavian settler in the vicinity of Dublin was uprooted in some orchestrated campaign of 'ethnic cleansing'; a more likely outcome of the attack would have been exile for the ruling elite and their followers.

It seems that Máel-Finnia and his surviving brothers maintained the policies of their father in the matter of relationships with the dominant Uí Néill dynasties. Without necessarily breaking links with Cenél nEogain, they concentrated more on cultivating ties with the powerful Clann Cholmáin dynasty, paramount kings of Uí Néill from the late ninth through most of the tenth century. It is possible that Máel-Finnia had some role in the arrangement whereby his brother Máel-mithig married Lígach (d. 922) daughter of Flann Sinna (d. 916) king of Tara, the mother of his son Congalach. The subsequent marriage of his daughter Der-bhFáil, to Donnchad Donn (d. 944) son of Flann Sinna, took place after his time. Presumably, they were not married until after 927, when Donnchad's previous wife, Caindech, died. Der-bhFáil herself, styled *regina Temrach* ('queen of Tara'), died in 931. These links,

---

dynasty, see A.P. Smyth, *Scandinavian York and Dublin: the history and archaeology of two related Viking kingdoms*, i (Dublin, 1975), 27, 29–30. **31** *AU* 902; on the expulsion of the Norse from Dublin, see ibid., 60–1; MacShamhráin, *The Vikings*, 51.

combined with the political impact of Máel-Finnia himself, may go some way towards accounting for the achievement of his nephew Congalach son of Máel-mithig, who emerged as successor to Donnchad Donn, when his dynasty had been excluded from the kingship of Tara for two hundred years.[32] Máel-Finnia, however, did not live to see any of these developments unfold; he died, prematurely it seems, in 903 and was succeeded as king of Brega by his brother Máel-mithig, who continued to support Clann Cholmáin and, from 916, the resurgent Cenél nÉogain interests.[33]

His obit for the year 903 provides the earliest indication of Máel-Finnia's ecclesiastical role. In the Annals of Ulster, he is styled (in addition to *Rex Breg*, 'king of Brega') *religiosus laicus*, which the editors translate as 'religious layman'; the implication seems to be that he retired to the religious life, although no specific ecclesiastical site is mentioned.[34] Significantly, the Annals of the Four Masters records for same year (s.a. 898 = 903) the obit of Máel-Findén (almost certainly the same person), styled *abb* (abbot; the Four Masters are inclined to 'modernize' or 'simplify' titles) and associated with Inis Pátraic. It is not clear whether he resigned his church position on succeeding to the kingship, retired to religion for the last year of his life (following the sack of the Dublin *longphort* in 902), or combined the role of king with that of superior of Inis Pátraic. Given the status of saint later accorded to him, the latter, on balance, appears the most likely.

Unfortunately, nothing is known of the circumstances in which Máel-Finnia became superior of Inis Pátraic – or of any previous association on the part of his lineage with that site. In fact, little is known of the earlier history of Inis Pátraic – beyond the case for its identification with the island attacked by the Vikings in 798. Whatever about its alleged

---

32 *AU* 956; death of Congalach; his achievement has been remarked upon, but not adequately explained; see Donnchadh Ó Corráin, *Ireland before the Normans* (Dublin, 1972), 19, 118; Byrne, *Irish kings*, 87. **33** *AU* 919 records the death of Máel-mithig at the battle of Islandbridge, supporting the Clann Cholmáin king of Mide Conchobar ua Máele-Sechnaill, and the king of Tara Niall Glúndub of Cenél nÉogain, against the returned Norsemen. **34** The term seems to mean something more than *laicus fidelis* ('faithful layman'), or *laicus monachus* ('paramonastic ecclesiastical dependent'); see Etchingham, *Church organisation*, esp. 306–8; note that *Airchinnech láich* ('lay superior') occurs in the Irish laws; *Corpus Iuris Hiberniae*, 2.4; see Fergus Kelly, *Guide to Early Irish Law* (Dublin, 1988), 42 n. 26.

Patrician origins (discussed above by Professor Thomas), Inis Pátraic appears to have had British associations, as with nearby Lusk and Bremore. The island is associated with St Do-Chonna – or Mo-Chonna – who is commemorated in the martyrologies on 13 January.[35] The surviving sources have reference to many saints so-named, suggesting that the original *persona* of Mo-Chonna (a hypochoristic, or 'pet', form of Colmán/Columba), has been the subject of major cult-fragmentation – giving rise to many variants of the name and numerous duplications. Also commemorated on the same date (13 January) are the similarly named To-Chonna of Cuairne (unlocated) and Mo-Chonna of Lemchoill (Lowhill, Co. Laois). The latter, in turn, appears to be the same as Mo-Chonna of Gallen, or Mo-Chonnóc son of Brychan king of Brycheiniog, otherwise known as Colmán *Brit*. In the light of recent thinking regarding cult-fragmentation,[36] it is not unreasonable to infer that Mo-Chonna of Inis Pátraic is identical to Colmán the Briton.

Although the later emergence of dynastic interests at Inis Pátraic is not reflected in the surviving record, it has been noted above that increased Síl nÁeda Sláine dominance of the area was, by the ninth century, accompanied by a shift in the abbatial succession at Lusk, while there are indications of some involvement there by Clann Chernaig Sotail of Southern Brega. That same lineage, it seems, had some devotion to Mo-Chonna; there is mention of one Gilla-Mo-Chonna (d. 1013), son of Fogartach, king of Deiscert Breg.[37] Such naming practices often point to a connection with the ecclesiastical site concerned (as with Máel-Finnia and his family's apparent link with Clonard). As it happens, that particular individual flourished a century later, and there is no evidence that the rival Clann Chernaig lineage had established interests at Inis Pátraic before the emergence of Máel-Finnia. However, whether or not it was the case that a rival Síl nÁeda Sláine segment, or any other dynastic group, was exercising influence at the site prior to c.868, it made sense for the family of Máel-Finnia, having just gained political power at the expense of cousins, to expand upon their local ecclesiastical connections.

35 *Fél. Óeng.* (notes); *Mart. Donegal*; see also the list of homonymous saints for Mo-Chonna Inse Pátraic, LL 368c 19; *Bk. Leinster*, vi, 1669. **36** See, for instance, Pádraig Ó Riain, 'Towards a methodology in Early Irish hagiography', *Peritia*, 1 (1982), 146–59. **37** *AU* 1013; see Rawl B 502, 144b 34; O'Brien, *Corpus Geneal. Hib.*, 161.

As remarked at the outset, the combination of kingship with ecclesiastical leadership roles is not unknown in the medieval Irish record; but Máel-Finnia is unusual in that he is featured in the martyrologies. Although he flourished too late to find a place in the earliest calendars, Máel-Finnia of Inis Pátraic is commemorated at 6 February in the twelfth-century Félire of Ua Gormáin and in the later Martyrology of Donegal. Such commemoration is generally a prerogative of sainthood, and on this account, he is accorded a brief 'life' in Colgan's, *Acta Sanctorum Hiberniae*. Generally, as already noted, 'saints in the Irish tradition' were church founders (or foundresses). Clearly, Máel-Finnia did not found the church of Inis Pátraic; that honour is ascribed to Do-Chonna. There may, however, be a case for re-foundation; it would not be inappropriate that a religiously inclined regional king, who had played a prominent part in breaking (at least for a time) Norse control of this area, should have re-established on a sound footing (if not rebuilt) an ecclesiastical centre which had perhaps declined due to pressure from Norse Dublin. Significantly, Ryan and his co-authors have drawn attention above to various features, which exist alongside the twelfth-century standing remains on Church Island, including an earthwork surrounding the church site and possible terracing on the shoreline. They consider the possibility of a tenth-century 'period of revival', which could indeed include work carried out in the time of Máel-Finnia or subsequently inspired by his achievement. As in so many such cases, further archaeological investigation is required.

Christian cults and cult centres in Hiberno-Norse Dublin and its hinterland

HOWARD B. CLARKE

By the year 1152, when Dublin attained archiepiscopal status that put it on a par with Armagh, Cashel and Tuam, there were an impressive number of churches in the walled town and its suburbs. Indeed, no place in Ireland had ever before accumulated so many cult centres – not even the biggest and most illustrious of the monasteries. These Dublin churches served the people of four discrete settlement nuclei (fig. 9.1): first, Áth Cliath, the aboriginal secular site on the ridge-top overlooking the eponymous ford across the river Liffey; secondly, Duiblinn, a former monastic site associated with early abbots and bishops; thirdly, Dyflinn, which had evolved from a Viking trading emporium into an Hiberno-Norse town; and fourthly, Ostmanby, the Hiberno-Norse transpontine suburb that had grown up probably in the eleventh century. A multiplicity of places of Christian worship is a characteristic of big towns and cities in medieval Europe. By the eleventh century we know that some of the larger English towns had numerous churches: Norwich, for example, may have had over forty in 1086.[1] Dublin was more comparable with Thetford in the same county, a town with at least thirteen churches and an estimated population of 4,000 to 5,000 at that time.[2] Many of these urban churches were probably *Eigenkirchen*, proprietory churches founded and patronised by members of wealthy trading families. Dublin, too, could have acquired some of its churches in this way. Unfortunately, we generally lack hard evidence. Only one Dublin church, Christ Church cathedral, has any kind of foundation narrative; for the most part we are left with a name (cult figure), a location and occasionally a little archaeological information. As a general rule, the more specific or unusual the cult, the less difficult it is to offer an explanation, but speculation will never be very far away.[3]

---

1 H.C. Darby, *Domesday England* (Cambridge, 1977), p. 305.   2 Ibid., p. 306.   3 Given the nature of this topic, there is a certain amount of overlap with an earlier essay that adopts a

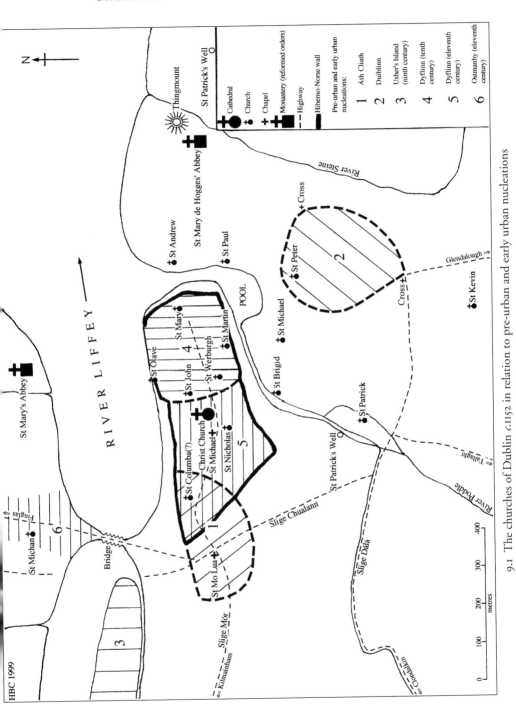

9.1 The churches of Dublin c.1152 in relation to pre-urban and early urban nucleations

According to the two late medieval accounts preserved in the Black Book of Christ Church, the secular founder of Dublin's first cathedral was King Sitriuc Silkbeard, who gave a site in the town along with gold and silver.[4] This site may have been cleared of earlier houses, similar to those outside the stronghold (*dún*) which had been burnt by the king of Tara (high-king) in 1015.[5] The extensive crypt, functional and undecorated in the earlier, eastern half, may have been necessitated both by the slope of the ground and by the presence of occupation debris. Recent archaeological investigations there have uncovered some masonry towards the west end. This has been interpreted variously as part of an earlier church, the base of a round tower, and reinforcement of the crypt itself.[6] According to the same late medieval accounts, Dublin's first Hiberno-Norse bishop, Dúnán (Latin Donatus), who was presumably an Irishman, built a nave, two collateral structures (probably aisles), a chapel dedicated to St Nicholas on the north side, and other buildings.[7] The cathedral's foundation is not recorded in any contemporary source, but probably dates from the period between Sitriuc's return from his Roman pilgrimage late in 1028 and his deposition as king in 1036.[8] The dedication to the Holy Trinity is a sign of external influence from Canterbury, whose cathedral likewise had the by-name Christ Church.

The first contemporary mention of Dublin's cathedral is contained in a poem preserved in the Book of Uí Maine, which stems from *c*.1121.[9] This is an Armagh product designed to promote that church's claim to

much longer perspective: H.B. Clarke, 'Conversion, church and cathedral: the diocese of Dublin to 1152' in James Kelly and Dáire Keogh (eds), *History of the Catholic diocese of Dublin* (Dublin, 2000), pp 19–50. **4** Aubrey Gwynn, 'Some unpublished texts from the Black Book of Christ Church, Dublin' in *Analecta Hibernica*, xvi (1946), p. 309. **5** *Chron. Scot.*, pp 254–5. For interesting speculations, see Roger Stalley, 'The construction of the medieval cathedral, *c*.1030–1250' in Kenneth Milne (ed.), *Christ Church cathedral, Dublin: a history* (Dublin, 2000), p. 55. **6** A further possibility is that Dúnán's episcopal palace was situated here, due west of his cathedral church (H.B. Clarke, *Dublin, part I, to 1610* (Irish Historic Towns Atlas, no. 11, Dublin, 2002), p. 29). **7** Gwynn, 'Some unpublished texts', p. 309. I have here followed Roger Stalley's suggested identification of these structures ('Construction of the medieval cathedral', p. 56). **8** *Ann. Tig.*, ii, 260; *Chron. Scot.*, pp 266–7. **9** Slightly earlier and later dates have been proposed (Martin Holland, 'Dublin and the reform of the Irish church in the eleventh and twelfth centuries', *Peritia*, xiv (2000), p. 136; Donnchadh Ó Corráin, 'Ireland, Wales, Man and the Hebrides' in Peter Sawyer (ed.), *The Oxford illustrated history of the Vikings* (Oxford and New York, 1997), p. 107). A shorter version of this poem, preserved in Lebor na cert (Book of rights), has been dated 1105 x 1152 (D.N. Dumville et al., *Saint Patrick, AD 493–1993* (Studies in Celtic History, vol. 13, Woodbridge, 1993), p. 264).

jurisdiction over the bishopric of Dublin and *ceall Crist* is included along with other churches in the town without any hint of its primacy.[10] Christ Church cathedral, of course, was a high-status place of worship and presumably the burial place of bishops and kings. A late medieval tradition preserved by James Ussher had it that Bishop Dúnán (d. 1074) was laid to rest at the right-hand side of the high altar; more recently it has been suggested that the first Irish under-king of Dublin, Murchad of Uí Chennselaig (d. 1070), was buried at the left-hand side.[11] The Christian cult figure linked to the cathedral from the very beginning, St Nicholas, was the patron of dioceses, merchants, and sailors among others. His cult was widespread in northern Europe by the twelfth century and urban churches dedicated to him often occupy central locations. The original chapel at Christ Church is referred to in a deed of 1541, as a cellar with a loft called St Nicholas's chapel.[12] Very possibly his cult was refocused in a separate building due south of the cathedral, perhaps in the twelfth century.

Another building linked to Bishop Dúnán in the Black Book is a chapel dedicated to St Michael the Archangel.[13] This was situated due west of the cathedral, in the episcopal palace, and was probably a private chapel for the bishop's own use, rather like the later chapel of St Sepulchre in the archiepiscopal palace near St Patrick's cathedral. We seem to sense that an episcopal complex was developing in the vicinity of the Hiberno-Norse cathedral, which would have been reinforced later in the century by the Benedictine priory established by Dúnán's successor.[14] St Michael was a cult figure who was venerated widely by both Christians and Jews from an early date. In the west he was regarded as the protector of soldiers in particular – a suitable provision in a town that would have seen itself as being constantly under threat from native Irish predators. Chapels dedicated to him were commonly built on hill-tops, the best known being Monte Gargano in southern Italy, Mont-Saint-Michel in north-

---

10 *Bk Uí Maine*, 126 b 56. 11 James Ussher, *The whole works of the Most Rev. J. Ussher …* , ed. C.R. Elrington (17 vols, Dublin, 1847–64), reprinted from *Veterum epistolarum Hibernicarum sylloge …* (Dublin, 1632), here at iv, 488; Seán Duffy, lecture delivered on 20 October 1998. 12 *Christ Church deeds*, ed. M.J. McEnery and Raymond Refaussé (Dublin, 2001), no. 1182. 13 Gwynn, 'Some unpublished texts', p. 308. 14 Aubrey Gwynn (ed.), *The writings of Bishop Patrick, 1074–1084* (Scriptores Latini Hiberniae, vol. 1, Dublin, 1955), p. 7.

western France, and St Michael's Mount in south-western England. Thus the ecclesiastical complex round Christ Church cathedral was of high status and was linked to kings, under-kings, bishops and merchants. There can be little doubt that it was essentially an Hiberno-Norse creation.

Turning now to the 'eastern core' of the Hiberno-Norse town, that is, to the site of the *dún* of the mid-tenth century, there appear to have been five churches two centuries later. Of these, two have relatively specific associations. St Olave's (Óláfr's) clearly has Scandinavian connotations, the cult being focused on the king of Norway who was killed in the battle of Stiklestad in 1030 (around the time of the foundation of the Hiberno-Norse diocese). By the following year Óláfr was being regarded in Norway as a Christian martyr and his cult spread far and wide in northern Europe. We find churches dedicated to him at Dublin and Waterford in the west and at Novgorod in the east. It is interesting that the earliest documented church at Dublin's sister-town of York, apart from the Minster, was also dedicated to St Olave.[15] According to the Anglo-Saxon Chronicle, this church was founded by Siward, earl of Northumbria (*c*.1033–55), a Danish appointee of King Cnut.[16] What was probably Dublin's closest trading partner at that time, Chester, also had a church with this distinctive dedication. Judging by its location down by the Liffey quayside, Dublin's church would have been frequented by sailors and traders plying the northern seas. Among the relics of Christ Church cathedral was part of the vestment of St Olave, possibly presented by Bishop Dúnán himself.[17] It is reasonably certain, then, that this church was founded in the mid-eleventh century, in an environment where the evidence of ship-building, wood carving and runic inscriptions points to a lively Scandinavian cultural presence.

The other church with specific associations is St Werburgh's, the cult figure being the daughter of a king of Mercia. During the ninth century her body had been translated to Chester in order to protect it from

---

15 A.P. Smyth, *Scandinavian York and Dublin: the history and archaeology of two related Viking kingdoms* (2 vols in 1, Dublin, 1987, reprinted from original ed. in 2 vols, Dublin and NJ, 1975–9), ii, 235. **16** *The Anglo-Saxon Chronicle: a collaborative edition*, vi, *MS D*, ed. G.P. Cubbin (Cambridge, 1996), p. 74. **17** *The Book of Obits and Martyrology of the cathedral church of the Holy Trinity, commonly called Christ Church, Dublin*, ed. J.C. Crosthwaite with introduction by J.H. Todd (Dublin, 1844), p. 141.

Viking predators.[18] Later, Werburgh became the patroness of that town's principal church and one-time cathedral (1075–1102).[19] This period of maximum prestige coincided with crucial developments in the Irish ecclesiastical reform movement, which culminated in the first synod of Cashel held in 1101. Aubrey Gwynn suggested dating limits of 1172 x 1178 for the establishment of this church in Dublin, but it could have been founded earlier.[20] Near the beginning of the tenth century there had been (enforced) secondary migration from Dublin to the Wirral peninsula due north of Chester, while the evidence of coins and pottery hints at regular trading contacts. It is a striking fact that several Chester-based moneyers of the tenth and eleventh centuries had Gaelic names, while the marten skins that constituted part of the burgesses' dues to the king of England are presumed to have come from Ireland, probably via Dublin.[21] The same burgesses are known to have been enjoying trading rights and privileges in Dublin no later than the reign of Henry I (1100–35).[22] St Werburgh's church at Dublin had parochial status early in the Anglo-French period, again pointing to a well-entrenched position by 1170.[23]

Two further churches in the eastern core of the town commemorated central figures in the life of Christ – Mary and John the Baptist. By the twelfth century the cult of Mary was widespread in western Europe, witness the dedication of Cistercian houses. Two monasteries belonging to reformed orders were founded at Dublin in mid-century and their dedications illustrate the same point: St Mary's abbey (1139) and St Mary de Hogges' abbey (c.1146).[24] A church in her honour (*ceall Muire*) is mentioned in the Armagh poem of c.1121 and must relate to a different

---

18 For a brief summary, see Donald Attwater, *The Penguin dictionary of saints* (London, 1965), p. 340.   **19** E.B. Fryde et al. (eds), *Handbook of British chronology* (3rd ed., London, 1986), p. 253.   **20** Aubrey Gwynn, 'The origins of St Mary's abbey, Dublin' in *RSAI Jn.*, lxxix (1949), p. 119.   **21** E.J.E. Pirie, *Sylloge of coins of the British Isles: Grosvenor Museum, Chester*, pt 1, *The Willoughby Gardner collection of coins with the Chester mint-signature* (London, 1964), pp 34–7; *Liber censualis vocatus Domesday Book*, ed. Abraham Farley (2 vols, London, 1783), i, fo. 262b1, 2. The farm of the borough consisted of £45 and three 'timbers' (*timbres*) of marten skins, which suggests that the importation of such skins was a long-standing arrangement. **22** R.H. Morris, *Chester in the Plantagenet and Tudor reigns* (Chester, n.d. [1893]), p. 480, no. 1; J.H. Round, *Feudal England: historical studies on the eleventh and twelfth centuries* (London, 1895; reprinted, with new pagination, 1964), pp 353–4.   **23** *Alen's reg.*, p. 29.   **24** At least to this extent, late Hiberno-Norse Dublin – a trading town with extensive overseas contacts – was caught up in 'the new spirituality of the twelfth century' (Henrietta Leyser, *Hermits and the new monasticism: a study of religious communities in western Europe, 1000–1150* (London,

site.[25] This may reasonably be identified as that of the church known from later records as St Mary del Dam, situated just inside the eastern gate of the town and due north of the castle. A pious Hiberno-Norseman called Gillamurri ('servant of Mary') occurs in the twelfth century and St Mary's may be an example of an *Eigenkirche*.[26] St John's, on the other hand, is not included in the poet's list, which cannot be regarded as necessarily complete. Gillamurri is known to have had a son named Gillamichell ('servant of Michael') and he is recorded as having granted St John's church to Holy Trinity cathedral, an act that is again suggestive of an *Eigenkirche*.[27] Its proximity to the cathedral bespeaks a founding family or individual of high socio-economic status. The focus on John the Baptist is perhaps redolent of a religious environment in which conversion to Christianity was still a current process, or at least a not-too-distant memory. Only later was the dedication revised to John the Evangelist, at a time when the gospel could be taken as having been heard on a regular basis.[28]

Least readily interpreted in this group of five churches is St Martin's, situated near St Werburgh's and coexisting with it for a time as an Anglo-French parish. The building was apparently located on a small bluff overlooking the pool of Dublin. The large quantity of bones and coffins found by chance at Darby Square in 1785 may well have represented its graveyard.[29] Churches associated with the evangelist of late Roman Gaul can be exceedingly early, as in the case of Canterbury. Tours, on the river Loire, was well known and had been on Columbanus's route bound for Ireland before he turned back towards the Continent at Nantes. The Life of St Martin by Sulpicius Severus had much influence on early Irish hagiography.[30] On balance, it is probable that a church situated in the eastern core of Viking Dublin postdates the initial construction of the *dún*. In that case we may be looking at a reflection of trading contacts with north-western France, as is evidenced by some of the pottery found

1984), p. 64 and passim). **25** *Bk Uí Maine*, 126 b 56. **26** *Alen's reg.*, p. 29. **27** Ibid. **28** Clarke, *Dublin, part I, to 1610*, p. 17 (by c.1285 at the latest). **29** John Bradley and H.A. King, 'Urban archaeology survey, part VIII: Dublin City' (unpublished report, 2 vols, n.d. [1988]), ii, 117. **30** Máire Herbert, 'The Life of Martin of Tours: a view from twelfth-century Ireland' in Michael Richter and J.-M. Picard (eds), *Ogma: essays in Celtic studies in honour of Próinséas Ní Chatháin* (Dublin, 2002), p. 76.

in excavations and by the foundation of St Mary's abbey in 1139 as a Savigniac house.[31] What is noticeable about all of the churches so far discussed, including St Martin's, is that none of them is directly associated by the name of the cult figure or by any process of formal dedication with Ireland itself. Three of the names were biblically derived (John the Baptist, Mary and Michael the Archangel), two were associated with fourth-century bishops (Martin and Nicholas), one was Scandinavian (Olave), one was Anglo-Saxon (Werburgh), and one was English-inspired (Holy Trinity). When we move outside the town defences, including the 'western extension' of the eleventh century, the picture becomes at once more diversified and more obscure.

Apart from the cathedral, only one of the secular churches at Dublin has a putative foundation date, this being 1095 for St Michan's supplied by Richard Stanihurst and borrowed by Meredith Hanmer.[32] In fact, the traditions about the origins of this church are complicated and it could have been founded as late as 1106.[33] Hanmer attributed the donation of the site itself to a Murchad, king of Leinster, perhaps in error for Muirchertach Ua Briain, the over-king of Dublin from 1094 to 1114. In that case, the year 1095 looks entirely credible in that it may represent the exercise of royal authority early in the new régime.[34] The establishment of this church implies that a population existed across the Liffey from the main town and may have been linked to the construction of the permanent bridge first securely documented in 1112.[35] The name of the cult figure was believed by Hanmer to have been Norse ('Danish'), perhaps because it was unusual. Ailbhe MacShamhráin has suggested that Michan may be a hypochoristic form of Cainnech (Mo Chainne), the patron of the monastery at Finglas, and indeed the Armagh poet does refer to a church of St Cainnech situated in the district north of Dublin.[36] The

---

31 P.F. Wallace, 'Anglo-Norman Dublin: continuity and change' in Donncha[dh] Ó Corráin (ed.), *Irish antiquity: essays and studies presented to Professor M.J. O'Kelly* (Cork, 1981), p. 253; Gwynn, 'Origins of St Mary's abbey', pp 110–25. **32** Meredith Hanmer, 'The chronicle of Ireland' in James Ware (ed.), *Ancient Irish histories: the works of Spencer, Campion, Hanmer and Marleburrough* (2 vols, Dublin, 1633; reprinted 1809), ii, 194. **33** Emer Purcell, 'Oxmantown, Dublin: a medieval transpontine suburb' (MPhil thesis, NUI Dublin, 1999), pp 17–18, 60–7. **34** Clarke, 'Conversion, church and cathedral', p. 39, n. 148. **35** *AFM*, ii, 994–5. **36** *Bk Uí Maine*, 126 b 53.

cathedral's own tradition was that Michan was an Irish saint, bishop and confessor, but there are no other references to him.[37]

When we move south-eastwards to the lower reaches of the river Poddle and beyond, a different balance of ecclesiastical associations is encountered. None of the churches in this district is documented before the twelfth century, though two of them have yielded a limited amount of archaeological evidence. Four of the cult figures recorded then and later are biblical, including St Peter. The church linked to his memory was situated, off-centre, inside a typical ecclesiastical enclosure still preserved in the street pattern.[38] Moreover recent archaeological investigations have uncovered two sections of a large ditch that may represent a smaller, inner enclosure round St Peter's church reminiscent of those at sites such as Kells and Kildare.[39] The main enclosure at Dublin measured approximately 335m by 260m and therefore belongs to the late Leo Swan's biggest size category.[40] Much later references to two stone crosses on opposite sides of the enclosure may be indicative of relict features of the early monastic phase.[41] This is the site that was probably associated with the abbots and bishops of Duiblinn recorded, however inadequately, in the period 633–790.[42] The cult of St Peter was known in Ireland from early times and would have been appropriate in a location near the convergence of long-distance overland routes across the island and of overseas contacts with Britain and the Continent.[43] Nevertheless the dedication familiar to us could have been Hiberno-Norse.[44] As at

---

37 *Book of Obits and Martyrology*, pp lxx, 149. **38** H.B. Clarke, *Dublin c.840 to c.1540: the medieval town in the modern city* (2nd ed., Dublin, 2002), large-scale map. **39** Tim Coughlan, 'Excavations at the medieval cemetery of St Peter's church, Dublin' in Seán Duffy (ed.), *Medieval Dublin IV: proceedings of the Friends of Medieval Dublin symposium 2002* (Dublin, 2003), pp 19–23, figs 5, 7, 8 and plate 1; Anngret Simms, H.B. Clarke and Raymond Gillespie (eds), *Irish historic towns atlas*, i (Dublin, 1996, separately paginated), pp 2, fig. 2 (Kildare), 3, fig. 1 (Kells). **40** Leo Swan, 'Enclosed ecclesiastical sites and their relevance to settlement patterns of the first millennium AD' in Terence Reeves-Smyth and Fred Hamond (eds), *Landscape archaeology in Ireland* (British Archaeological Reports, British Series, vol. 116, Oxford, 1983), p. 274 and fig. 4. **41** *Registrum prioratus Omnium Sanctorum juxta Dublin*, ed. Richard Butler (Dublin, 1845), p. 30 (c.1267); *Anc. rec. Dublin*, i, 157 (1328, then known as the Butter Cross). **42** For discussion and references, see Clarke, 'Conversion, church and cathedral', pp 23–9 and fig. 1. **43** John Ryan, 'The early Irish church and the see of Peter' in J.A. Watt, J.B. Morrall and F.X. Martin (eds), *Medieval studies presented to Aubrey Gwynn, S.J.* (Dublin, 1961), pp 3–18; R.D. Edwards, *An atlas of Irish history* (2nd ed., London and New York, 1981), p. 190, fig. 57. **44** An approximate date of 1100 has been suggested on archaeological grounds (Coughlan, 'Excavations at St Peter's church', p. 26).

Armagh, Kells and other places in Ireland, a memory of the ancient monastery was retained centuries later, as the road system that evolved in the Anglo-French city went around rather than across the enclosure site and the parish of St Peter was demarcated by precisely the same boundary.

The Armagh poem refers to a church at Dublin dedicated jointly to Saints Paul and Peter (*ceall Poil is Pedair*).[45] These two central figures in the Bible story were often linked in the Middle Ages because they shared the same feast-day, 29 June. No such church at Dublin is otherwise on record, but a new stone church with this dual dedication was consecrated at Armagh itself by Archbishop Cellach in 1126.[46] This was a new-style abbey that stood apart from the cathedral there and later joined the Arroasian congregation. It was probably founded a few years before 1126 and is thus in conformity with the presumed date of the poem. The northern author could have been mistaken, or perhaps was endeavouring to make Dublin seem as Armagh-like as possible. According to Archbishop John Alen, writing in the early sixteenth century, there had been a church of St Paul near the river Poddle and therefore not far distant from St Peter's. The site was then a garden.[47] Like St John's, St Paul's was granted by Gillamichell the Hiberno-Norseman to Holy Trinity cathedral and thus was probably an *Eigenkirche* by origin.[48] The dedication to a major biblical figure with a distinctive personal conversion story may well have appealed to converts in the Hiberno-Norse town. The biblical Paul was buried on the site of the church of that name outside the walls of ancient Rome, a not dissimilar location to that of the church at faraway Dublin many centuries later.

The same Armagh poem refers to a church of St Michael situated south of the *dún*, which could well have been that known to later generations as the church of St Michael le Pole ('of the pool').[49] This church had a round tower, as we see on De Gomme's map of 1673 and in two eighteenth-century drawings.[50] An excavation conducted in 1981

---

45 *Bk Uí Maine*, 126 b 54–5. **46** *AU*, pp 570–1. **47** *Alen's reg.*, p. 293. **48** Ibid., p. 29. **49** *Bk Uí Maine*, 126 b 52. **50** Reproduced conveniently in H.B. Clarke, Sarah Dent and Ruth Johnson, *Dublinia, the story of medieval Dublin* (Dublin, 2002), p. 47 (de Gomme); Clarke, 'Conversion, church and cathedral', figs 4, 5 (drawings).

led the archaeologists to believe that this tower had stood inside the main body of the building, rather like St Kevin's church at Glendalough.[51] The foundation levels of both church and tower were dated to the twelfth century, but underneath were burials of the late tenth or early eleventh century.[52] These burials in turn concealed earlier human activity dating back to the eighth century.[53] Clearly, therefore, this was an ancient site, going back to a time in the Viking period when both pagan and Christian burial practices could have coexisted. The Hiberno-Norse name that we have already encountered, Gillamichell, hints at the cult of St Michael in a familial or personal context and St Michael's could have been yet another *Eigenkirche* at Dublin. The round tower may have been erected as some kind of status symbol, as Dublin Christians sought to imitate those of neighbouring communities such as Swords. Sited by the pool that may have sheltered the local fleet, this feature may also have served as a watch-tower, just as classic round towers were capable of fulfilling more than one function at a time.[54]

Finally in this biblically-derived group of cult figures there was St Andrew, whose church was located outside the east gate on the right bank of the Poddle. The cult of St Andrew was well established in Scotland by the ninth century and its observance at Dublin could be a sign of Meic Ottair or Meic Torcaill patronage in the mid-twelfth century. These families supplied a number of under-kings of Dublin, the last of whom, Asculf mac Torcaill, may well have passed by this church as he made his escape by ship in September 1170 and as he made his fateful return journey in May of the following year.[55] Perhaps symbolically, the ultimate winner of the great contest for mastery of Dublin, King Henry II of England, is said to have spent the winter of 1171–2 in

---

51 Margaret Gowen, 'Excavations at the site of the church and tower of St Michael le Pole, Dublin' in Seán Duffy (ed.), *Medieval Dublin II: proceedings of the Friends of Medieval Dublin symposium 2000* (Dublin, 2001), pp 39–40, 50. **52** The western boundary of an apparently large cemetery associated with this church has been identified on the eastern side of Bride Street (Mary McMahon, 'Early medieval settlement and burial outside the enclosed town: evidence from archaeological excavations at Bride Street, Dublin' in *RIA Proc.*, cii C (2002), pp 77–82. A significant number of curved roof tile fragments, possibly associated with the church itself, were also recovered (ibid., pp 82–3, 97–8). **53** Gowen, 'Excavations at the site of St Michael le Pole', pp 28–32, 48. **54** Clarke, 'Conversion, church and cathedral', pp 45–6. **55** Giraldus Cambrensis, *Expugnatio Hibernica: the Conquest of Ireland*, ed. A.B. Scott and F.X. Martin (A New History of Ireland, Ancillary Publications, vol. 3, Dublin, 1978), pp 68–9, 76–7.

a specially constructed wattle palace in the vicinity of St Andrew's church.[56]

Four further cult figures linked to sites on this side of the defended town were all Irish. Most obscure is St Máel-Ruain's, said by the Armagh poet to have been situated with St Michael's south of the *dún*.[57] Such a church is nowhere else recorded at Dublin, but Máel-Ruain had been a major figure in the *célí Dé* movement of the late eighth century centred on Finglas and Tallaght.[58] The cult was therefore a local one and was perhaps given recognition for a time in an Hiberno-Norse *Eigenkirche*. On the other hand, the poet makes no mention of St Kevin's, a dedication that must represent an association of some kind with Glendalough. Ailbhe MacShamhráin has suggested that this cult was encouraged by Uí Briain over-kings of Dublin in the late eleventh and early twelfth century.[59] At the time of the reforming synod of Ráith Bressail conventionally dated to 1111, the Hiberno-Norse diocese of Dublin was apparently subsumed into that of Glendalough; this may have presented the monks there with a suitable opportunity to establish a base outside the town's defences. In the papal confirmation of *c*.1179 St Kevin's is described as a *villa*, that is, an estate or manor that may have supported visitors from the monastery in the mountains.[60] By 1226 there was a suburban market near this church, which lay just outside the liberty boundary established probably at the time of Henry II's over-wintering at Dublin.[61] A base situated near a thriving town would have given the monks access to non-local goods being traded there. The Armagh poet does make reference to St Brigid's church (*ceall Brigdi*), though he mistakenly places it inside the defences.[62] Like Máel-Ruain, Brigid was a locally-derived cult figure from that part of Leinster which was controlled for a long time by segments of Uí Dúnlainge.[63] Apart from this indication of its existence,

56 *Chronica Magistri Rogeri de Houedene*, ed. William Stubbs (4 vols, Rolls Series, vol. 51, London, 1868–71), ii, 32. **57** *Bk Uí Maine*, 126 b 52. **58** Peter O'Dwyer, *Célí Dé: spiritual reform in Ireland 750–900* (2nd ed., Dublin, 1981), *passim*. The Armagh poet seems to have had in mind a location nearer to Dublin than Tallaght itself, though from a distant northern perspective the latter could have been deemed to be south of the *dún* of Dublin. **59** A.S. MacShamhráin, *Church and polity in pre-Norman Ireland: the case of Glendalough* (Maynooth Monographs, vol. 7, Maynooth, 1996), p. 212. **60** *Alen's reg.*, p. 7. **61** *Cal. doc. Ire., 1171–1251*, pp 203, 204. **62** *Bk Uí Maine*, 126 b 56–7. **63** F.J. Byrne, *Irish kings and high-*

the earliest piece of documentary information that we have is that St Brigid's was granted to Holy Trinity cathedral by the last Hiberno-Norse under-king, Asculf (1160–70).[64] Once again, therefore, we may be contemplating an *Eigenkirche*.

St Brigid is a largely legendary figure, but the ambitions of the church of Kildare and of its Leinster patrons had caused her cult to spread far and wide. Like St Patrick, Brigid is claimed to have made provincial circuits of parts of Ireland and on her second journey, centred on Brega and Mide, she allegedly came into personal contact with Patrick himself.[65] And so we come ourselves to the question of the cult of St Patrick at Dublin. By a nice irony, a church of St Patrick was founded a short distance upriver from St Brigid's south of the main town site. It is duly mentioned in the Armagh poem (*ceall P[hádraig]*).[66] The cult must go back earlier to at least the previous century, for Dublin's second Hiberno-Norse bishop was Gilla-Pátraic ('servant of Patrick', latinised as Patricius) and his dates are 1074–84. According to the English evidence, soon after Bishop Dúnán's death the clergy and people of Dublin wrote to Archbishop Lanfranc as their metropolitan.[67] They said that they had selected the priest Patrick, a man of noble birth and character, as their preferred choice as bishop. In his letter to King Gofraid (Gothricus) of Dublin, Lanfranc comments that Patrick had been brought up in monastic institutions since boyhood, though he does not say where.[68] We know from Patrick's own poems that he was trained as a Benedictine monk at St Mary's priory, Worcester.[69] When examining the latinity of Bishop Patrick's writings, Ludwig Bieler detected what he termed 'a certain "Hibernian" flavour' and observed that the native (Irish) tradition of Latin learning was not yet extinct.[70] If Gilla-Pátraic was a local boy made good, his particular choice of personal devotion was presumably made

---

kings (London, 1973), p. 150. **64** *Alen's reg.*, p. 29. **65** Kim Mc Cone, 'Brigit in the seventh century: a saint with three lives?' in *Peritia*, i (1982), pp 122–3. **66** *Bk Uí Maine*, 126 b 51. **67** Gwynn, *Writings of Bishop Patrick*, p. 2. **68** Ibid., p. 6; Helen Clover and Margaret Gibson (eds), *The letters of Lanfranc archbishop of Canterbury* (Oxford, 1979), pp 68–9: 'monasticis institutionibus a pueritia enutritum'. The Annals of St Mary's abbey attribute the choice to the king, with the assent of the people and clergy (*Chartularies of Saint Mary's abbey, Dublin*, ed. J.T. Gilbert (2 vols, Rolls Series, vol. 80, London, 1884), ii, 249; Martin Holland, 'The synod of Dublin in 1080' in Seán Duffy (ed.), *Medieval Dublin III: proceedings of the Friends of Medieval Dublin symposium 2001* (Dublin, 2002), p. 81). **69** Gwynn, *Writings of Bishop Patrick*, pp 6–7, 10–11, 104–5. **70** Ibid., p. 48.

---

before he went to England. Conceivably the cult could have gone back to the days of Brian Bórama, who was the overlord of Dublin in the latter part of his reign and who was doubly related by marriage to King Sitriuc. Brian made a well-publicised visit to Armagh and his body was taken there after his death at Clontarf.[71] During Bishop Patrick's pontificate (1080), an abbot of Armagh appears to have participated in the high-king's visit to Dublin, bearing the famous Staff of Jesus as the insignium of his ecclesiastical superiority.[72] In 1105 his successor, Domnall mac Amalgada, was taken seriously ill whilst engaged in a peace-making exercise at Dublin.[73]

Against this background a church associated with St Patrick, and perhaps representing the Armagh interest, was established at an unknown date. Relics of its burial ground in the form of six graveslabs belonging to the Rathdown group, dated roughly to the tenth and eleventh centuries, still survive in the present cathedral.[74] Located on a damp but well-defined island between two branches of the river Poddle, we peer dimly through the historical mist at an Armagh presence on the periphery of a settlement occupied by independent-minded craftsmen and traders, whose ecclesiastical loyalty was normally given to Canterbury.[75] When the opportunity arose after Bishop Samuel's death in 1121, Dublin's supposed links with the national apostle were elaborated in Armagh's favour. Similar notions were articulated in the 1180s by Jocelin of Furness, who has St Patrick make a triumphal progress to Dublin.[76] Jocelin was in the business of assisting the *conquistador* John de Courcy in promoting Downpatrick as the major cult centre in the north. There the new cathedral was equipped with the unbeatable combination of the

---

71 *AU*, pp 434–5, 448–9. The body was handed over to the Armagh clerics at Swords, then a church on the border of Fine Gall and Brega (Edel Bhreathnach, 'Columban churches in Brega and Leinster: relations with the Norse and the Anglo-Normans' in *RSAI Jn.*, cxxix (1999), pp 9–10). **72** *Ann. Tig.*, ii, 305–6; *Chron. Scot.*, pp 292–3. For the date, see Holland, 'Synod of Dublin', pp 85–7. **73** *AU*, pp 544–5. **74** Heather King, 'The pre-1700 memorials in St Patrick's cathedral' in Conleth Manning (ed.), *Dublin and beyond the Pale: studies in honour of Patrick Healy* (Bray, 1998), pp 82–4. **75** For the suggestion that the promotion of this cult may have been 'a part of Dublin's quiet aspiration to be the metropolitan see of all Ireland', see Holland, 'Dublin and reform', p. 136. **76** Thomas Messingham (ed.), *Florilegium insulae sanctorum; seu, vitae et acta sanctorum Hiberniae* (Paris, 1624), p. 33; E.L. Swift (trans.), *The life and acts of Saint Patrick, the archbishop, primate and apostle of Ireland* ... (Dublin, 1809), p. 84. For a detailed analysis of the two versions of this story, see Holland, 'Dublin and reform', pp 137–40.

purported relics of no fewer than three 'national' saints – Patrick, Brigid and Columba.[77]

We come finally to the question of the cult of Columba, the Latin form of Colum Cille. Once again we have tantalising hints of the presence of a church at Dublin with this dedication. Early in the Anglo-French period its priest, called Richard, witnessed an important document in the company of many other priests in the town.[78] There is no further reference to a church with this dedication and Aubrey Gwynn guessed, perhaps rightly, that it was soon afterwards refounded as St Audoen's.[79] Accordingly we can work only backwards from this point. In 1127 the shrine of Colum Cille at Skreen in Co. Meath was stolen by the Hiberno-Norsemen of Dublin and then returned within a month;[80] this incident may suggest a certain regard for the cult on their part, if a somewhat irregular one. A few years earlier the Armagh poet started off his list of churches at Dublin with the church of the sons of Áed (*ceall mac nÉda*), which precedes St Patrick's and was presumably of some importance.[81] Is there an echo here of the inscription on the base of the shrine of the Cathach of Columba, where we are told that the maker was Sitriuc mac Meic Áeda?[82] A man called Mac Aedha features in the so-called Irish 'charters' preserved in the Book of Kells and is there described as a *cerd*, 'metalworker' with particular reference to gold and silver.[83] The shrine is conventionally dated to 1062 x 1098 and is usually assumed to have been made at Kells, still the headquarters of the

77 Giraldus Cambrensis, *Expugnatio*, pp 234–5, 353, n. 479. For a fuller discussion with valuable references, see Raghnall Ó Floinn, 'Insignia Columbae I' in Cormac Bourke (ed.), *Studies in the cult of Saint Columba* (Dublin, 1997), pp 140–2.   **78** *Christ Church deeds*, no. 364; H.J. Lawlor, 'A calendar of the *Liber Niger* and *Liber Albus* of Christ Church, Dublin' in *RIA Proc.*, xxvii C (1907–9), p. 24, no. 42.   **79** As reported in G.A. Little, *Dublin before the Vikings: an adventure in discovery* (Dublin, 1957), pp 116–17 and n. 49. The argument based on evidence from Dublin's hinterland, north and south, that the Hiberno-Norsemen had been active in promoting the cult of St Columba (Bhreathnach, 'Columban churches in Brega and Leinster', passim) makes it all the more probable that the same cult figure had been patronised in the town itself.   **80** *AFM*, ii, 1026–7.   **81** *Bk Uí Maine*, 126 b 44.   **82** H.J. Lawlor, 'The Cathach of St Columba' in *RIA Proc.*, xxxiii (1916–17), p. 391 (appendix by E.C.R. Armstrong).   **83** Ibid.; John O'Donovan, 'The Irish charters in the Book of Kells' in *The miscellany of the Irish Archaeological Society*, i (Dublin, 1846), pp 140–1; Gearóid Mac Niocaill (ed.), *Notitiæ as Leabhar Cheanannais, 1033–1161* (Galway, 1961), pp 22–3; Bairbre Nic Aongusa, 'The charters in the Book of Kells: a historical analysis' (MPhil thesis, NUI Dublin, 1989), p. 95. Mac Niocaill makes a tentative association between the Mac Aedha of the charter and the maker of the shrine (*Notitiæ as Leabhar Cheanannais*, p. 22, n. 1: 'b'fhéidir gurb é seo

9.2 View of the ecclesiastical remains at Swords, Co. Dublin; S. Hooper (1792)

Columban federation.[84] It belongs to the group of metal artefacts that shows the strongest Scandinavian influences.[85] Conceivably there was a church at Dublin that was being patronised as an *Eigenkirche* by members of this particular family. Sitriuc's hybrid name is suggestive of intermarriage and his family could have been variously based at both Kells and Dublin. On this interpretation, admittedly highly tenuous, this Dublin church was linked to the cult of St Columba.[86]

Observance of this cult at Dublin can be traced back to the previous century for, as is well known, King Amlaíb Cúarán died as a penitent on

an duine a rinne cumhdach do Chathach Cholaim Chille'). **84** Lawlor, 'Cathach of St Columba', p. 392, being the dates of Domnall mac Robartaigh as coarb of Kells. It could even have been made in Dublin itself in the time of Bishops Patrick and Donngus. **85** Raghnall Ó Floinn, 'Schools of metalworking in eleventh- and twelfth-century Ireland' in Michael Ryan (ed.), *Ireland and insular art, AD 500–1200* (Dublin, 1987), pp 180–1. **86** These

Iona in 981, whither he had sought refuge after his decisive defeat at the battle of Tara in the previous year.[87] Charles Doherty has suggested that Columban clergy had been active in seeking converts in Dublin in the tenth century, while Edel Bhreathnach sees a role for Amlaíb in founding or patronising the church at Skreen as part of a programme of territorial expansion in the district.[88] There are contrary indicators: in 969 Amlaíb's son, Sitriuc (the future king), plundered Kells jointly with the king of Leinster, and the old freebooter himself drove cattle away from the same monastery in the following year, again with the help of Leinster allies.[89] Doherty has identified ambivalence as a personal trait of Amlaíb Cúarán – a quality that was surely passed on to his son Sitriuc.[90] The most proximate centre of Columban influence was Swords, which is first reliably documented in relation to St Columba in 994 when it was burnt by King Máel-Sechnaill of Mide.[91] This deed was committed probably in retaliation for a plundering expedition in the previous year by the Dublin Norsemen and, if that is the case, it implies that Swords was perceived as part of Fine Gall, the territory of the foreigners.[92]

Much further back in time, around the year 635, a monastery with Columban associations had been founded on the island of Rechru.[93] This insular foundation has to be understood in the context of ecclesiastical administration by another, far-distant insular foundation – Iona.[94] Assuming that the location was indeed Lambay Island, the cult had had a presence in the Dublin area for a long time by the tenth century. Possibly Swords was developed as a more convenient land-based

suggestions are offered in place of the defeatist 'pure invention' of the earlier essay (Clarke, 'Conversion, church and cathedral', p. 45). **87** *Chron. Scot.*, pp 226–7; *AFM*, ii, 710–13. On the wider background to the king's retirement to Iona, see Bhreathnach, 'Columban churches in Brega and Leinster', pp 9–10. **88** Charles Doherty, 'The Vikings in Ireland: a review' in H.B. Clarke, Máire Ní Mhaonaigh and Raghnall Ó Floinn (eds), *Ireland and Scandinavia in the early Viking Age* (Dublin, 1998), pp 299–301; Edel Bhreathnach, 'The documentary evidence for pre-Norman Skreen, County Meath' in *Ríocht na Midhe*, ix, no. 2 (1996), pp 41–3; idem, 'Columban churches in Brega and Leinster', pp 10–11. **89** *AFM*, ii, 692–3; *AU*, pp 408–9; *Chron. Scot.*, pp 218–19. **90** Doherty, 'Vikings in Ireland', pp 304–5. **91** *AU*, pp 424–5. **92** Nevertheless, 'Swords in the eleventh and twelfth centuries belonged to a thoroughly Irish ecclesiastical milieu' (Bhreathnach, 'Columban churches in Brega and Leinster', p. 13). **93** *AU*, pp 118–19. **94** Michael Byrnes, 'The Árd Ciannachta in Adomnán's *Vita Columbae*: a reflection of Iona's attitude to the Síl nÁeda Sláine in the late seventh century' in A.P. Smyth (ed.), *Seanchas: studies in early and medieval Irish archaeology, history and literature in honour of Francis J. Byrne* (Dublin, 2000), pp 132–3, 135–6.

centre on what was then the northern border of the Scandinavian kingdom of Dublin. It is notable that, when the diocese of Glendalough was defined territorially in the early twelfth century, its north-eastern pole was Lambay, which had been granted to Holy Trinity cathedral by the Uí Chennselaig under-king, Murchad, in the third quarter of the eleventh century.[95] The north-western pole was Greenoge, on the Broad Meadow Water, which I suspect was the northern limit of Hiberno-Norse settlement until well into the twelfth century.[96] Both Lambay and Swords were included in the foundation-circuit of Columba in the Irish Life composed probably in the mid-twelfth century (fig. 9.2).[97]

Accordingly, the cult of Columba could have been observed at an early stage in pre-Viking Áth Cliath, but there is no firm evidence. The church site later occupied by St Audoen's was, I believe, undoubtedly early to judge by the morphology of that part of the city, though we still lack archaeological confirmation.[98] The second site that we can be reasonably confident was pre-Viking is St Peter's. These two locations represent the duality of Áth Cliath and Duiblinn. There may have been other cult centres, but of these we have no proof. The settlement of pagan Scandinavians created a hiatus, though many of the local people, particularly the womenfolk, may well have continued to practise Christianity. During the tenth century Christian cults probably started to establish or to re-establish themselves, initially in peripheral locations relative to the emerging town, such as St Michael's and St Patrick's. A critical mass of adherents must have been reached by *c*.1030, hence the foundation of a cathedral church. Thereafter the defended town and its immediate surroundings were colonised by an eclectic mix of cult centres, reflecting the diversity of contacts and influences in Dublin

---

95 *Alen's reg.*, p. 28.   96 See further Clarke, 'Conversion, church and cathedral', p. 37 and nn 129–30.   97 Máire Herbert, *Iona, Kells, and Derry: the history and hagiography of the monastic familia of Columba* (Oxford, 1988), p. 315.   98 For the topographical context, see Clarke, *Dublin c.840 to c.1540*. Stone foundations and traces of a possible boundary wall have been found (Linzi Simpson, 'Forty years a-digging: a preliminary synthesis of archaeological investigations in medieval Dublin' in Seán Duffy (ed.), *Medieval Dublin I: proceedings of the Friends of Medieval Dublin symposium 1999* (Dublin, 2000), pp 37–8). The extant grave-slab, belonging to the so-called Rathdown group, could have originated nearby, though its previous history is unknown.

relative to Ireland and to places abroad. No single cult predominated, for the cathedral had a theologically-derived dedication. Only in the Anglo-French period, whether by accident or by design, was one of this plethora of cult figures elevated above all the others, namely St Patrick, and even he had to make do with a soggy suburban locale down by the river Poddle.

The twelfth-century reform and Inis Pátraic[1]

MARTIN HOLLAND

In the year 1148 a number of bishops and priests assembled for a synod on the island known as Inis Pátraic, off the coast of the modern town of Skerries to the north of Dublin. This synod had been summoned by St Malachy, then papal legate in Ireland. At the time, the structural reform of the Irish church, begun thirty-seven years earlier at the synod of Ráith Bressail, had as yet to be brought to a successful conclusion. Papal approval for decisions made there had still to be obtained as some problems remained to be resolved. As a result of decisions made at the synod of Inis Pátraic, however, that approval would shortly afterwards be forthcoming. Because of that it would be true to say that these decisions had consequences for the church that last up to the present day. The main problem facing the synod revolved around the situation of the diocese of Dublin. For a number of years there had been a struggle between Dublin and Armagh which had seen Dublin omitted from the new hierarchy that had been set up at Ráith Bressail. A compromise was achieved at Inis Pátraic which paved the way for Dublin to take its place within that hierarchy and for papal approval to be won finally for the new structure of the Irish church.

---

1 The sources used in the preparation of this paper may be found in M. Holland, *The introduction of a new organizational structure to the Irish church (1072–1152)*, (unpublished PhD dissertation, University of Dublin, 2003). See also idem, 'Dublin and the reform of the Irish church in the eleventh and twelfth centuries', *Peritia*, 14 (2000), 111–60. On the general topic of Irish church reform in this period: A. Gwynn, *The twelfth-century reform*, A history of Irish Catholicism II (Dublin & Sydney, 1968); idem, *The Irish church in the eleventh and twelfth centuries*, ed. G. O'Brien (Dublin, 1992); K. Hughes, *The church in early Irish society* (London, 1966); J.A. Watt, *The church in medieval Ireland* (2nd ed. Dublin, 1998); idem, *The church and the two nations in medieval Ireland* (Cambridge, 1970); the Introduction in H.J. Lawlor (tr.), *St Bernard of Clairvaux's Life of St Malachy of Armagh* (London, 1920); Marie Therese Flanagan, *Irish society, Anglo-Norman settlers, Angevin kingship* (Oxford, 1989) 7–55; M. Holland, 'The synod of Dublin in 1080', Seán Duffy (ed.), *Medieval Dublin III* (Dublin 2002), 81–94.

To understand the significance of the compromise achieved, it is necessary to examine the struggle that went on between Armagh and Dublin in the years preceding the synod. In the year 1074, Bishop Patrick was consecrated for the see of Dublin. He was consecrated in London by Archbishop Lanfranc of Canterbury and gave a profession of obedience to him. In that profession of obedience Dublin is described as the '*metropolis*' of Ireland ('*metropolem Hiberniae*'). As the word '*metropolis*' is used here in an ecclesiastical setting it is best translated as 'metropolitan church'. Patrick's profession of obedience to Lanfranc, therefore, refers to Dublin, or more correctly, to the Dublin church as the 'metropolitan church of Ireland'. This description is no mere accident. There is other, even more clear, evidence for its use in relation to Bishop Patrick's consecration. This is to be found in the standard type letter or *decretum* which was purportedly sent by the clergy and people of Dublin to Lanfranc requesting him to consecrate Patrick. The use of such a *decretum* strongly suggests that it did not come from Dublin but was in fact prepared at Canterbury. In this *decretum* the church of Dublin is described as the metropolitan church of the island of Ireland. This confirms the description of the Dublin church, as found in the profession of obedience that Patrick made. It makes clear that the Dublin church is being described as the metropolitan church of the whole island of Ireland. This claim has been seen as preposterous since Irishmen of the day would have looked upon Dublin as 'the city of the foreigners' and could not imagine it as being the 'metropolis of Ireland'. Because of this historians have tended to dismiss it. However, the claim was clearly made and has therefore to be taken seriously. What is more it seems most likely to have been the first of a series of events which would ultimately see the *pallium*, the sign of papal approval, given to Bishop Gréine in 1152, thus making him the first canonical archbishop of the metropolitan see of Dublin. And it had even more important consequences than that. By stating that the Dublin church was the metropolitan see of the whole of Ireland it set the scene for a clash with Armagh whose island-wide authority it challenged. It is most likely that it was responsible for drawing Armagh into the arms of a reform movement that was to emerge, particularly in Munster.

When Lanfranc consecrated Bishop Patrick and got a profession of obedience from him it is clear that he saw Dublin not just as the metropolitan see of the whole of Ireland but as being a metropolitan see under his primacy. The second half of the eleventh century saw a number of primacies being founded or re-founded in many continental countries. In England after the Norman conquest something similar was afoot. Lanfranc, the new archbishop of Canterbury, was striving to impose his primacy over the metropolitan see of York. As part of that struggle we gain an insight into his plans for Ireland. In the year 1072, two years before he consecrated Bishop Patrick, he wrote to the pope in relation to his dispute with York; in this he said 'my predecessors exercised primacy over the church of York and the whole island which men call Britain and over Ireland as well'. Two years later when he consecrated Patrick it became clear how he would exercise that primacy. He would exercise it through the see of Dublin. It would become the metropolitan see for the whole ecclesiastical province of Ireland. As well as his own province of Canterbury he would exercise his primacy over two other provinces, each with a metropolitan, one at York, the other at Dublin.

Of course it was only a plan, perhaps even a mere aspiration, at this stage. After all Patrick, whom he consecrated, was merely a bishop not an archbishop. That would have required papal approval and the granting of a *pallium*. But the Dublin church of 1074 could not, by any stretch of the imagination, be seen to have already achieved a relationship with the rest of the Irish church that would justify it being granted metropolitan status with authority over the whole Irish church. As a plan, however, it made some sense and was perhaps the only option open to Lanfranc if he were to take the claim to primacy over the Irish church seriously. However, he would have to proceed with caution so as not to alienate the Irish church. We can see this caution in the way he addressed a senior Irish bishop, Domnall Ua hÉnna, and a number of clergy who were assembled with him. This is contained in a letter he wrote to them. He calls them his 'dearest brethren, whom I love as a father'. Nowhere in this letter does he refer to himself as their primate. His approach to them is sensitive and not assertive.

The same approach would be expected of the man charged with the task of giving some meaning to the title of metropolitan church of the island of Ireland. And it would appear that Bishop Patrick did succeed in giving some element of meaning to that title during his pontificate even if it is not clear how that meaning was perceived by Irish authorities, both secular and ecclesiastical, outside the Dublin church. How else can one explain the calling of a synod in Dublin in 1080 by the most powerful Irish king of the day, Tairdelbach Ua Briain, and his subsequent participation, together with Irish bishops, alongside the clergy and people of Dublin, in electing Bishop Patrick's successor and sending him to Canterbury for consecration? If the new bishop was to be the bishop of Dublin only, why not leave his election to the clergy and people of that see only? Did their participation signify a perception on their part that the bishop of Dublin had a greater role in Irish church affairs than that of being merely bishop of Dublin? This question cannot be answered but there is an implication that such a perception did exist. If such were the case it would have been due to the efforts of Bishop Patrick.

While Lanfranc was treading cautiously with the Irish clergy outside Dublin, he was relating more actively with the church of Dublin. It is known that he sent books, vestments and church ornaments to Patrick's successor, Bishop Donngus, for use by the church of Dublin. Furthermore, and more importantly, Lanfranc was most likely responsible for the installation of a chapter of monks from Canterbury at the cathedral in Dublin during the pontificate of either Patrick or Donngus. This was an important move and would be entirely in keeping with his plan to exercise Canterbury's primacy over Ireland through the agency of a metropolitan see based in Dublin. It is most likely that some formal link between that chapter and Canterbury was maintained after its foundation. Such a link would have been an important vehicle for ensuring that Canterbury's interests continued to be articulated in Dublin. It would also ensure that Canterbury was kept abreast of events in Dublin. It would be particularly important during vacancies in the see of Dublin. It would provide a mechanism through which Canterbury could exercise influence over the selection of successor bishops in Dublin. Above all it would ensure the continuation of the link between Canterbury and Dublin.

While Donngus was bishop of Dublin, Lanfranc died in May 1089. After a vacancy that lasted for four and a half years he was succeeded as archbishop of Canterbury by Anselm. Some time after his consecration Anselm wrote to all the canonical bishops in Ireland informing them of his election. In this letter he says that he feels duty bound to remind them to be vigilant and severe in dealing with anything which they find in their regions which is contrary to ecclesiastical doctrine. However, anything that they are unable to resolve locally he urges them to bring it to his notice. This letter is certainly written from the perspective of one who sees himself as having pastoral responsibility for the whole of Ireland. That would suggest that Anselm saw Canterbury as still holding the primacy over the whole of Ireland even if he did not expressly say so. On the other hand, his closest companion at Canterbury, Eadmer, never hesitates in openly expressing this claim. However, like Lanfranc before him Anselm is cautious about implementing Canterbury's primacy through the agency of a metropolitan see in Dublin. This can be detected if one examines the order in which he places the names of the bishops to whom he addresses the letter. He places Domnall Ua hÉnna's name ahead of the bishop of Dublin. He was obviously being tactful. There was nothing to be gained by arousing the antagonism of a prelate as important as Ua hÉnna.

Samuel was the only bishop of Dublin whom Anselm consecrated. His *decretum* has not survived. However, we do know from Eadmer's *Historia Novorum* that one did exist. In this we also read that Muirchertach Ua Briain, king of Munster and aspirant to the high-kingship of Ireland, took part in Samuel's election just as his father had taken part in the election of his predecessor Donngus. It is likely also that the clergy referred to in Eadmer's report include Irish bishops as was the case at the election of Donngus and at that of Máel-Ísu, the first bishop of Waterford.

Whatever about Anselm's caution in dealing with Irish bishops outside Dublin it would appear that Canterbury's plan for Ireland, as set out by Lanfranc, was still in place. Early in his pontificate Bishop Samuel carried out metropolitan duties in a discreet manner. In the same year in which he was consecrated bishop of Dublin he was instrumental in setting up a new bishopric at Waterford and having its first bishop Máel-Ísu sent to Canterbury for consecration. This is clear from an analysis of the evidence which survives. That evidence comes from two sources. The first is Eadmer's *Historia Novorum*. The second is a letter sent by Walkelin, bishop of Winchester, to Anselm. According to Eadmer, two separate letters were sent to Anselm from Ireland. The first was a petition to Anselm 'in right of the primacy he held over them and of the apostolic authority which he exercised' to erect a bishopric in Waterford. The second, which Eadmer publishes in full, is a *decretum* for the consecration of Máel-Ísu. However, there is a necessary difference between it and all other contemporary *decreta*. In a normal *decretum* the first part is concerned with the fact that a vacancy has occurred in a particular see. This is the justification for the request that the person elected be consecrated, a request that comes in the second part. Quite obviously in a situation like that of Waterford, where a new bishopric is being set up, one cannot speak about a vacancy having occurred. The first part of a normal *decretum* cannot therefore be used. Instead it is replaced by a preamble which, while tailored to suit a new bishopric, uses a justification similar to that of a normal *decretum*. The second part however is in line with a normal *decretum* in use at Canterbury at the time. It is simply an abbreviation of that *decretum* and it does not omit anything of essence. The fact that it comes from a Canterbury source cannot be in doubt as a textual comparison between it and those contemporaneously in use at Canterbury shows. The similarity between them could suggest that Máel-Ísu's *decretum* was drawn up at Canterbury when he arrived there for consecration, despite Eadmer's statement that he was sent from Ireland with a *decretum*. However, the subscriptions on the *decretum* which include King Muirchertach Ua Briain, his brother and a number of Irish bishops argues against that. Even the possibility that Eadmer may have himself entered these names along with the statement that there were 'many more signatories whom for brevity we have thought it unnecessary to name' in order to give support to his often stated claim of Canterbury's primacy over all of Ireland, is countered by the one other piece of evidence that is available. This makes it clear that Máel-Ísu was elected in Ireland. The letter which bishop Walkelin sent to Anselm tells us that 'the king of Ireland with the bishops and clergy and people of that country' elected Máel-Ísu. Furthermore, it tells us that the initiative in terms of the practicalities associated with the consecration were taken in Ireland. We can feel sure, therefore, that Eadmer is telling the truth when he says that Máel-Ísu was sent to Canterbury with the *decretum*. Accepting that this Canterbury *decretum* was prepared in Ireland, the question to be asked then is: who was likely to have had access to such a *decretum*? The answer to this must surely be Samuel who was himself consecrated at Canterbury the previous Easter. As well as that he had a monastic chapter in Dublin founded most likely by Canterbury monks and in possession of books sent from Canterbury to Dublin. And of course we have direct evidence that Samuel was indeed involved since he signed the *decretum* along with the others.

It is likely therefore that Samuel, in the early months of his pontificate, was instrumental not alone in organizing the election and consecration of Máel-Ísu but also in setting up the new diocese of Waterford. By so doing he was taking a step towards implementing the plan, as originally conceived by Lanfranc, that Dublin would be the metropolitan see for the whole of Ireland. And judging from the precedence in the list of episcopal signatories to Máel-Ísu's *decretum*, he was doing it with the unknowing co-operation of Irish bishops but not in a way that asserted the position to which his see aspired. Just as in the case of Anselm's letter to Irish bishops, precedence was conceded to Irish bishops. This was probably done to gain their co-operation and to prevent antagonizing them. It does not mean that the aspiration or the plan had disappeared – far from it as Samuel's actions were soon to show. For some reason, possibly to do with the character of his personality, Samuel exposed the plan for all to see. We know this from two letters written by Anselm, one to Máel-Ísu, the other to Samuel. Both refer to Samuel behaving like a metropolitan. What Anselm has to say requires close study. He writes: 'Moreover I have heard that you cause a cross to be carried before you on the way. If this is true, I command you to do so no longer since it is applicable only to an archbishop who has been confirmed with the *pallium* by the Roman pontiff.' This reprimand by Anselm makes it clear that what is wrong with Samuel's behaviour is that he is acting as if he has already been confirmed as an archbishop by the granting of the *pallium* by the pope. He is not being reprimanded for acting as an archbishop *per se*. Quite clearly Samuel had not yet got a *pallium* from the pope and should not therefore have behaved as he did. The reprimand does not mean that Anselm was against the plan for the see of Dublin. Only when that plan had reached fruition could a *pallium* be applied for and presumably acquired. Only then could a Dublin prelate have the cross carried before him.

Both of these episodes – the erection of the new Waterford bishopric at Samuel's instigation and the carrying of a cross before Samuel – show that Lanfranc's plan was still alive. There is one further indication that that was the case: if Dublin was to have any hope of gaining metropolitan status over all of Ireland it would somehow have to show that it had a connection with St Patrick who had brought Christianity to Ireland. And so, despite its historical impossibility, Dublin invented a legend which purported to tell how St Patrick had converted the inhabitants of Dublin to Christianity. This legend was later to be re-invented by Armagh and used as proof that Dublin, since it was supposedly converted by Patrick, was in fact subject to Armagh.

It is not clear when or by what means Muirchertach Ua Briain became aware of Canterbury's plan in Ireland for the see of Dublin. In the year 1096 he participated in the election of both Samuel and Máel-Ísu and their dispatch to Canterbury for consecration. It is not clear whether he knew about Canterbury's plan at that stage. He could have co-operated with the elections while knowing the plan. If that is the case then he was about to change his mind. Alternatively he was in ignorance of it and soon afterwards found out about it and rejected it. Whichever was the case, his concept of how the Irish church was to be reformed was soon to become manifest. This concept saw reform taking place within a totally Irish context. There was no place in it for Canterbury.

The evidence for this is twofold. First, there is the synod of Cashel in 1101. Second, there is the entrance of Armagh into the drive for reform. The synod of Cashel came together at the command of Muirchertach. Decrees from the synod are recorded among the Ua Briain genealogies. However, the most important impetus for reform at the synod is not to be found in the decrees but rather in the action of Muirchertach Ua Briain. This action is the granting of Cashel to the church. It is widely reported in the annals. Most of them have one thing in common. The grant is made, not to some local community, but to all the christian people in Ireland. Cashel of the kings, which till then had no ecclesiastical connections of any substance, was to become the property of the whole church in Ireland forever. What this was to mean would become very clear only ten years later when Cashel was chosen at the synod of Ráith Bressail, at which Muirchertach Ua Briain was once again present, as the metropolitan see of the southern part of Ireland. The action must be seen as substantial and even dramatic and as an indication that Muirchertach already had in mind, in some form, the shape which the Irish church would take when it was reformed. That shape did not include Canterbury.

The first thing that had to be done in order to realize this reform was to bring Armagh, the most important ecclesiastical establishment in Ireland, into the reform movement. Fortunately for Muirchertach his family had a good relationship with Armagh. However, at the time of the synod of Cashel the *comarbae* of Patrick (i.e. the abbot of Armagh) was Domnall, a member of the Clann Sínaich. This family had controlled the coarbship of Patrick since the middle of the tenth century. Domnall was married and was not in holy orders. This obviously presented a problem for Muirchertach as such a situation was not compatible with the type of reformed church he was likely to have had in mind. He would have to persuade Armagh that a change was needed there. That would have presented Armagh with a great difficulty as it would mean changing a longstanding tradition. Muirchertach would need more than his persuasive powers if he were to have any hope of success in bringing about change in Armagh. He would need some strong leverage. That leverage was Dublin and the role that was planned for it in Ireland by Canterbury. Should this role come to pass, it would see Dublin usurping a situation in the Irish church which Armagh would have strongly believed belonged to it. Muirchertach would have had the opportunity to apply this leverage when he visited Armagh in 1103. He stayed there for a fortnight. And it would seem that he was successful in winning Armagh over to reform. For there can hardly be any other explanation for the abrupt change that was about to take place in Armagh. The revelation, by Muirchertach, of the plan for Dublin must have alarmed authorities in Armagh and aroused them to action. It is likely that nothing could be done in relation to the ecclesiastical status of the current *comarbae*, Domnall, as long as he lived. But the speed with which his successor, Cellach, assumed holy orders after his succession to the coarbship in 1105 would suggest that such action was planned in advance of his appointment. Cellach took orders a mere six weeks after the death of his predecessor. And in the following year, perhaps only a few months later, he was consecrated bishop, significantly while on a visit to Munster.

Although there is no hard evidence to prove that Muirchertach acted in the way that has just been outlined it seems to be the most likely way of explaining how Armagh was converted so suddenly to the side of reform. Of course, Armagh could have been alerted to Dublin's plan independently of Muirchertach. However, its interpretation of it and, much more importantly, the manner in which it should respond points to the reforming hand of Muirchertach. Of one thing we can be almost certain: the decision of a member of the Clann Sínaich to take orders was not spontaneous. The spur to Armagh's action in joining the reform movement was its acquiring the knowledge of Dublin's aspiration. This becomes manifest in later times as the conflict between Armagh and Dublin, which begins when Armagh discovers what is happening, is played out in public, particularly at crucial times like the selection of Samuel's successor.

With Armagh on board the reform movement, an alliance for reform was forged between the top ecclesiastic in Ireland and the most important king in Ireland. Forming an alliance for reform, however, was one thing; putting it into practice was quite a different matter. The problem must have been how one should go about it. It is clear that an analysis of how the church might be restructured was needed. Cellach, the new bishop of Armagh, was unlikely to have had the capacity to tackle that problem. The bishops who had attended the synod of Cashel were also unlikely candidates given their performance at that synod. Muirchertach would have had to look elsewhere for someone to tackle the problem. The person chosen was a man called Gille or Gilbertus in Latin. Given that this man became bishop of Limerick, the headquarters of Muirchertach Ua Briain, we can be in no doubt that it was Muirchertach himself who was most influential in choosing him for the task.

The first known fruit of Gille's work is a tract called *De statu ecclesiae*. He appended a letter to this tract which he addressed to all the bishops and presbyters of Ireland. It may be assumed, therefore, that the tract was prepared for a widespread circulation in Ireland. In it an overview is given of the structure of the whole church and the duties of its various members. It may be seen as preparing the way for the reforms that were to be proclaimed at the subsequent synod of Ráith Bressail, over which Gille himself presided. That he presided over that synod as papal legate is particularly significant. His firm belief in a unified church clearly governed by a hierarchy from the pope downwards, and his fervent advocacy of subjection to the apostolic see, as shown in both his tract and the letter which accompanied it, made him a suitable candidate for appointment as papal legate. However, we know almost nothing about the pope's involvement with the reform of the Irish church at this stage, although his appointment of a legate suggests that he had an active involvement. It seems reasonable to assume that he would not appoint a legate to preside over a synod unless he first knew what was to be discussed at that synod. That would suggest that he agreed, in principle, that the Irish church should have its own primate and hierarchy. It remained for the synod to flesh out the details. In this the pope differed from the view he held regarding both the Scottish and the Welsh churches. The former he believed should be subject to York, the latter to Canterbury and to each in its capacity as metropolitan.

At the synod of Ráith Bressail plans were drawn up for a hierarchy within the Irish church. There were to be two metropolitan sees, one at Armagh, the other at Cashel. The suffragan sees under each metropolitan bishop were outlined. However, there was one clear omission from the list of dioceses spelled out there. That omission was Dublin. As has already been noted, Dublin had its own plan and that was to become the metropolitan see for the whole of Ireland under the primacy of Canterbury. What was happening at Ráith Bressail was, therefore, a direct challenge to Dublin's plan. Given that Bishop Samuel of Dublin had been openly behaving as if he were already a metropolitan it is highly unlikely that he would have attended the Ráith Bressail synod even if he was invited. To do so would have meant giving up Dublin's ambition. His unwillingness to take part in the reform of the Irish church, completely within an Irish context, must be seen, therefore, as the reason why Dublin was omitted from the list of dioceses put forward at Ráith Bressail.

But it seems clear that the synod left the door open for the future entry of the Dublin diocese into the Irish church hierarchy. According to Geoffrey Keating, who had access to a record of the synod no longer extant, the synod chose as a model for the Irish hierarchy that which had originally been proposed for Canterbury and York. According to that model there would be two metropolitan provinces, each having an archbishop with twelve suffragans under him. In other words there would be thirteen bishops including the archbishop in each province – twenty-six bishops in all. At Ráith Bressail it was decided that, likewise, there would be two metropolitan provinces in Ireland, one for the northern part of the island, the other for the southern part. However, when it came to enumerating the bishops, their dioceses and boundaries only twenty-five were listed, thirteen in the northern part and twelve in the southern part, both including the archbishop. If the synod had set out to use the original Canterbury/York model and if it had been determined to keep Dublin out of the system for all time, it seems logical to expect that they would have outlined thirteen dioceses in each province. They did not do that. There can, therefore, be no doubt that it was their intention that Dublin should be included at some future time. How to achieve that would, of course, be the problem. Perhaps it was hoped that when the current bishop died an opportunity would present itself. And it would seem that that was what was behind the actions taken by Cellach when Samuel died in 1121. Evidence for the conflict between Armagh and Dublin, which up to this date can only be derived indirectly from its impact upon the reform movement, now becomes fully visible. According to the Annals of Ulster when Samuel died Cellach, the *comarbae* of Patrick, 'took the bishopric (of Dublin), by choice of the Foreigners and the Irish'. This is the first evidence we have of an attempt being made by a member of the newly created Irish church hierarchy to incorporate Dublin into that hierarchy. Efforts to persuade Dublin to become part of that system may have been made in the meantime. If so, they plainly failed. The list of dioceses prepared at Ráith Bressail included thirteen for the northern part of the island and twelve for the southern. The place retained for the future incorporation of Dublin was therefore in the southern province. That being the case, one might have expected Máel-Ísu of Cashel to take over the bishopric of Dublin when Samuel died, thus completing his full total of twelve suffragans. However, that did not happen. It was Cellach of Armagh who took the initiative. The reason for this seems to be quite clear. The threat posed by Dublin to Armagh's pre-eminent position in the Irish church had brought Armagh into the reform movement in the first case. That threat still existed. Only two years before Samuel's death Ralph d'Escures, archbishop of Canterbury, restated Canterbury's claim 'to the primacy of the whole of Britain as well as of Ireland' in a letter to the pope. As well as that, the implementation of Ráith Bressail's decrees must still have appeared quite fragile in 1121, only ten years after the synod. This is particularly so given the sudden illness, in 1114, of one of the main architects of that reforming synod, Muirchertach Ua Briain and his subsequent death in 1119. Furthermore a new power in the land, Tairdelbach Ua Conchobair, took control of Dublin from 1118. This was not merely symbolic control. It was something which Armagh had to take seriously, since Ua Conchobair took Dublin's side in the conflict with Armagh. It is for those reasons that it was Cellach and not Máel-Ísu of Cashel who seized the opportunity given by the death of Samuel and took over the bishopric of Dublin.

There was, however, resistance to this in Dublin. Eadmer tells us that Gréine was 'elected by the king and clergy and people of Ireland to the episcopacy of the see of Dublin'. He went to England to be consecrated by the archbishop of Canterbury. However, a certain cleric accompanied by a layman also travelled to England to try and prevent the consecration from going ahead. They argued that Gréine had not been elected 'by those to whom the power of that election most greatly belonged'. However, they lost the argument, according to Eadmer, because of the contents of the letter which Gréine brought with him and which was covered by the seal of the church of Dublin. In this letter, addressed to Archbishop Ralph, those who had elected Gréine give their reason for sending him to Canterbury for consecration. They state: 'For we always gladly subjected ourselves to the rule of your antecedents from which we remember we have received ecclesiastical dignity. Indeed, let it be known to you that the bishops in Ireland have great jealousy towards us, and especially that bishop who lives in Armagh, because we do not wish to comply with their arrangement but wish always to be under your lordship. For that reason we humbly seek your assent in order that you may promote Gréine to the sacred rank of episcopacy, if you wish to retain that diocese for a further period than the long time we have preserved it for you.'

From Eadmer's report it would appear that members of the Irish church were aware of the election of Gréine in sufficient time to send representatives to Canterbury to try and prevent the consecration of Gréine. That would suggest that he was elected after Cellach had taken over the bishopric. This, in turn, would explain what Cellach's initial action was intended to achieve. It may have been intended to influence the choice of Samuel's successor and to have him consecrated in Ireland and thereby accept the new hierarchical church there. With the election of Gréine, that initial aim failed. Representatives were therefore sent to Canterbury to try and stop the consecration from going ahead. And the argument used by these representatives is particularly important. It is based upon an understanding of where the power to elect Gréine lay. There existed, according to them, people with a greater power of election than those who had elected him. The address to Archbishop Ralph, in the letter which Gréine brought with him, would suggest that he had been elected by 'all the burghers of the city of Dublin and the whole assembly of the clergy'. The representatives of the Irish church who went to Canterbury would have argued that the greater power of election lay ultimately with the archbishop of Cashel. That was the thinking on the matter of episcopal election in the newly reformed church in Ireland at the time as can be seen in the tract which Gille had written for the synod of Ráith Bressail. Canterbury would, of course, have rejected this as it would have perceived itself to have had 'the greater power of election' in this case since it claimed primacy over all of Ireland and in a particular way over Dublin. This episode was a direct clash between Canterbury and the newly established Irish hierarchy.

However, it is important to note that there is no evidence that the Irish bishops elected and consecrated a bishop in Dublin in opposition to Gréine. This would suggest that, despite Cellach's action in taking over the Dublin see, the reformers wished to retain good relations with Canterbury, while at the same time asserting that it was they who had the 'greater power of election' when bishops for the see of Dublin were to be elected. Nevertheless, the pro-Canterbury people of Dublin obviously felt themselves to be under pressure. The core of the letter, which Gréine brought with him, reflects that. It contains a very clear and concise statement of the actual position of the newly reformed Irish church's relationship to Dublin, albeit from a Dublin perspective. Its perception of the situation is that the bishops of Ireland but especially the bishop 'who lives in Armagh' are paying particular attention to Dublin and perhaps applying pressure on it. The reason why they are applying that pressure is to get Dublin 'to comply with their arrangement'. That means, when decoded, that they are applying pressure because they wish to bring Dublin into the church structure that they had set up at Ráith Bressail.

However, the people of Dublin who sent Gréine to Archbishop Ralph for consecration were not prepared to go along with their wish. And given what we know about Ralph's views about the relationship between Canterbury and Ireland it was entirely predictable that he would accede to the request to consecrate Gréine. And so Gréine was consecrated bishop of Dublin and made a written profession of obedience to Canterbury. However, when he returned to Dublin he found that Cellach was still in possession of that see. He was banished and returned to Archbishop Ralph with whom he remained until Ralph died in 1122.

It seems reasonably clear that Cellach must have had support in Dublin. Otherwise he would not have been able to prevent Gréine from taking up his position in Dublin. Eadmer, no supporter of Cellach, admits that he had support. However, that support was by no means complete. He lacked the support of one very important man in particular; Tairdelbach Ua Conchobair, king of Connacht, king of Ireland 'with opposition' and, since 1118, king of Dublin did not support him. We know this from a letter sent by Henry I to Archbishop Ralph concerning the consecration of Gréine.

It is not known how long Cellach stayed in Dublin. The indications are, however, that he may have left in 1122 or even in 1121 while Gréine was residing with Archbishop Ralph. With Cellach no longer in Dublin, an opportunity must have arisen for Gréine to take up his office. And he may have been helped by Tairdelbach Ua Conchobair to do that. There is no evidence, however, that any agreement on this was arrived at between Armagh and Dublin. In fact, it is highly unlikely that any arrangement was made between them. Dublin remained firmly outside the newly established Irish hierarchy. The reason we can say this is to be found in the refusal of Pope Innocent II to grant *pallia* for Armagh and

Cashel to the great reformer, St Malachy, when he sought them in Rome in 1140. Innocent approved the foundation of a new metropolitan see at Cashel and he appointed Malachy as legate in place of the ailing Gille. However, in regard to the *pallia*, the pope said to Malachy: 'More formal action must be taken regarding the *pallia*. You are to call together the bishops and clergy and nobles of your country and hold a general council. Once all the people agree, you will request the *pallium* through trustworthy persons and it shall be given to you'. The key word here are 'once all the people agree'. The inference to be drawn from these and the refusal to meet Malachy's request for the two *pallia* is that all did not agree at the time Malachy made his request and that the pope knew it. Malachy's request to the pope was based upon the church structure decided at Ráith Bressail. But we have seen that the attempt of the reformers to incorporate Dublin into that structure led to open conflict and rebuttal of their attempt by Dublin and Canterbury. And it is most likely that Dublin's refusal to join in still remained in 1140 when Malachy went to Rome. All, therefore, were not in agreement at the time and the pope did not feel justified in giving the *pallia* to Malachy despite his high regard for him as is obvious from his appointing him as papal legate.

We know little about what happened after Malachy returned to Ireland. He was now papal legate and charged by the pope to get agreement from all before another attempt was made to seek the *pallia* from Rome. The most obvious obstacle in the path of such an agreement was Dublin. There was also the new power in the land, Tairdelbach Ua Conchobair, who in 1121 had been in opposition to the reformers. However, there must have been a growing awareness in Dublin of the lack of progress of its fundamental aim – to become the metropolitan see for the whole of Ireland under the primacy of Canterbury. As well as that, there must have been an awareness, as time went by, that the diocesan structure decreed at Ráith Bressail was not going to disappear even if it had not as yet gained full papal approval by the granting of the *pallia*. Furthermore, Malachy was now papal legate charged by the pope to get agreement of all so that those *pallia* would be given. This was a clear indication to Dublin that the pope wished to have a diocesan system within an Irish context only.

Papal approval had already been given for the two metropolitan sees of Armagh and Cashel. This meant that the possibility of Dublin getting papal approval as metropolitan of the whole of Ireland no longer existed. Dublin was left with no option but to salvage what it could from its aspirations. In doing so it would, somehow, have to come to terms with the new Irish diocesan system. It would appear, however, that it was determined to retain, as it would have seen it, its status as a metropolitan see. But given the situation it found itself in, it was no longer feasible to expect that the whole island would be its province. It would have to be satisfied with less. That was the compromise that was likely to have been negotiated by Malachy when he assembled bishops and clergy on Inis Pátraic in 1148. We have no direct evidence that Gréine attended the synod. However, we do have direct evidence that the question of how the *pallia* were to be obtained from the pope was discussed there and since that was of supreme importance to the bishop of Dublin, at the time, it is most likely that he did attend. Also there is evidence that Malachy most likely joined Gréine in Dublin in the same year for the consecration of the ground upon which St Mary's abbey was built. There was, therefore, no personal animosity between them that might have prevented him from attending. Given that he had the motivation to be there he is very likely to have attended. And indeed the outcome of the synod would suggest that he, in fact, did attend.

The choice of location for the synod appears to be somewhat peculiar – a small island off the coast. However, there may have been specific reasons for choosing it. It is near Dublin and decisions about the future of the see of Dublin would be taken at the synod. At the core of those decisions was the resolution of the conflict that had existed for some time between Dublin and Armagh. That resolution would see the primacy of Armagh being accepted by Dublin. That such acceptance should take place on an island associated with Patrick would have special symbolism for Armagh. It would be as if the acceptance had taken place in Armagh itself.

According to the sources, Malachy was sent by the synod to the pope to get *pallia* for Ireland. None of the sources tell us what the outcome of the synod was. However, this can be deduced from the number of *pallia* which Cardinal Paparo brought with him to Ireland four years later. It would appear that the Cistercian Pope Eugenius III accepted the decisions of the synod. Because of this it must be assumed that a final agreement was reached on the structure of the church during the synod. That, after all, was what Pope Innocent II, eight years earlier, had told Malachy was needed in order that *pallia* be given by Rome. Rome was now prepared to grant the *pallia* and Pope Eugenius sent Cardinal Paparo to Ireland bringing with him four *pallia*. This is a very significant fact as it has to be remembered that a *pallium* is a vestment worn by an archbishop. It is therefore a physical item. So before Paparo left Rome, if he were to bring four *pallia* with him, it would have to be already known and agreed that there would be four archbishops. In other words it was already decided. It was not a decision that was taken subsequently at the synod of Kells. The place where the final decision was made was Inis Pátraic in 1148, a decision which was subsequently approved by the pope.

One of the *pallia* which cardinal Paparo brought with him was for Tuam and it would appear that agreement that it would gain metropolitan status had been achieved some time before the synod of Inis Pátraic met. This was the culmination of a period during which Connacht had stood apart from the reform movement. It is most unlikely that any clergy from there had attended the synod of Ráith Bressail. As well as that we have already seen that Tairdelbach Ua Conchobair took a stand against the reformers in 1121. Furthermore, there is some evidence of continuing difference between that clergy of Connacht and the reformers in 1134. However, by 1140 it seems that dialogue between them was underway. Nevertheless, given that the dioceses in Connacht, which emerged from the synod of Kells in 1152, were changed more radically from those proposed at Ráith Bressail than those in any other part of Ireland it is clear that the original proposals were not satisfactory to the clergy of Connacht. There was much, therefore, to be negotiated between the two parties. Added to that, there was Ua Conchobair's prestige in the country at the time which would have made it imperative that he be won over to the side of reform. If the price of that was the granting of metropolitan status to Tuam, then it was a price that would have to be paid. If such a price could be paid to bring Dublin into the Irish diocesan structure and end Canterbury's pretensions, then it could be done to get the king of Ireland 'with opposition' and the Connacht clergy to accept the new reforms. And it would appear that agreement had been reached over the new status of

Tuam in the year before the synod of Inis Pátraic met; this would indicate that that synod had to deal with the problem of Dublin only.

The synod of Inis Pátraic paved the way for Gréine to become the first canonical archbishop of Dublin. It marks the point at which Dublin had achieved the recognized status of a metropolitan see, recognized by the rest of the Irish church and recognized shortly thereafter by the papacy. It was not, however, the kind of metropolitan see that Lanfranc had envisaged for it. But its determination to be a metropolitan see, initially under the primacy of Canterbury and finally under the primacy of Armagh, played a crucial role in stimulating the Irish church into reforming itself. Probably the most important part it played in the whole process was to jolt Armagh into the acceptance of the need to respond to the challenge it presented and to have that response channeled into reform by the shrewd manipulation of Muirchertach Ua Briain.

Contributors

Charles Thomas, CBE, FBA, Hon. MRIA: since 1993, Emeritus Professor of Cornish Studies, University of Exeter. Has a particular interest in early Christian history and archaeology, notably of Britain and Ireland in their European setting, and is the author of numerous works on this topic.

Edel Bhreathnach: research fellow at Mícheál Ó Cléirigh Institute for the Study of Irish History and Civilisation, University College Dublin. Formerly Tara Research Fellow, the Discovery Programme. Has many publications to her credit, including *Tara: a select bibliography* (Dublin, 1995) and is editor of *Tara: kingship and landscape* (forthcoming).

Catherine Swift: research fellow, Centre for Human Settlement and Historical Change, NUI Galway. She has published a number of papers – historical and archaeological – on themes relating to the early Irish church and society and is the author of *Ogam stones and the earliest Irish Christians* (Maynooth, 1997).

Cormac Bourke: curator of medieval antiquities at the Ulster Museum, Belfast. His many publications relate mostly to saints' cults and relics. He is the author of *Patrick: the archaeology of a saint* (Belfast, 1993) and is editor of *Studies in the cult of St Columba* (Dublin, 1997).

Peter Harbison: archaeologist at the Royal Irish Academy, where he is honorary academic editor, has produced numerous papers in the field of Irish archaeology, while his books include *Pre-Christian Ireland* (London, 1988), *A guide to the national monuments in the Republic of Ireland* (new ed. Dublin, 1992), and *The golden age of Irish art* (London, 1999).

Michael Ryan: Director of the Chester Beatty Library and President of the Royal Irish Academy, has published widely on archaeological topics. Among other works, he is editor of *The illustrated archaeology of Ireland*

(1991) and joint author of *Reading the Irish landscape* (2001), while his collected essays were published in 2002 as *Studies in Medieval Irish metalwork.*

Of his co-authors, Kevin Mooney is senior lecturer in and Frank Prendergast is head of the Department of Geomatics, Dublin Institute of Technology, while Barry Masterson formerly worked with the Discovery Programme.

Howard Clarke: Department of Medieval History, University College Dublin, where he is associate professor. He has numerous publications to his credit, many on settlement themes, and is co-editor of the *Irish historic towns atlas.* He is editor of *Irish cities* (Cork & Dublin, 1995), and co-editor of *Ireland and Scandinavia in the early Viking age* (Dublin, 1998).

Martin Holland: holds his doctorate from Trinity College Dublin. He has contributed papers relating to eleventh- and twelfth-century ecclesiastical history to *Peritia*, to Seán Duffy (ed.), *Medieval Dublin III* (Dublin, 2002), and to Routledge's *Medieval Ireland: an encyclopedia* (forthcoming).

Ailbhe MacShamhráin: lectures on the Medieval Irish Studies Programme at Department of Old and Middle Irish, NUI Maynooth, and is research fellow on the Monasticon Hibernicum Project funded by the Irish Research Council for the Humanities and Social Sciences. He has published several papers on early Irish political and ecclesiastical history and is author of *Church and polity in pre-Norman Ireland* (Maynooth, 1996) and *The Vikings: an illustrated history* (Dublin, 2002), and associate editor of Routledge's *Medieval Ireland: an encyclopedia*, ed. Seán Duffy (forthcoming).

Figures and tables

Figures and tables

TABLES

Index